A CLEAR VIEW

3 Steps to Unleashing the Power
of a Positive Self-Image

Also By Michael B. Ross:

Overcoming the Character Deficit

A Better Life Podcast

A CLEAR VIEW

3 Steps to Unleashing the Power
of a Positive Self-Image

MICHAEL B. ROSS

Mainstream Media by Woodchuck Arts
EAST LIVERPOOL OHIO

Mainstream Life Solutions
50404 Calcutta Smith Ferry Road
East Liverpool, Ohio 43920

Printed in the United States of America

Book edited by Woodchuck Arts, LLC.
Book design by Woodchuck Arts, LLC.

ISBN-13: 978-1518819445 (Mainstream Life Solutions)
ISBN-10: 1518819443

Praise

The book is an amazing roadmap to creating a positive self-image that will change you forever. If you follow the steps in this book you will truly unveil the gifts that you have to offer this world. God created us all as his masterpieces and this book will guide and give you the tools to fulfill your purpose in life.
- **Erik Klein, CEO, Klein's Corporations**

A Clear View was very inspirational. Michael motivated me to be a better person by giving me ways to overcome a negative self-image.
- **Paige, age 14**

A Clear View is an inspiring book that lays out a path to creating a strong and positive self-image. Michael has shown me that my self-image doesn't just affect me, but everyone around me. This book has opened my eyes to the power of self-image. *A Clear View* is a wonderful book that will impact it's readers tremendously.
- **Julia, age 15**

Michael is continuously looking for the answer to free us from the prison of our own mind. The key to finding our true value and personal freedom is by speaking value into others. When we speak low value to others, we are making a withdrawal from our own system of values. By serving others with a positive attitude, we also fuel the inner spirit of ourselves. Michael demonstrates how to rebuild our foundation that becomes damaged and torn down by so many others who do not value themselves.
- **Mark Lamoncha, CEO, Humtown Products**

In *A Clear View*, Michael Ross not only diagnoses the self-image problem that's stealing our potential, but he provides a practical prescription for overcoming it as well. *A Clear View* is a must read for teens and parents, as well as business owners, and team members to help us all reach a better life.
- **Brian Karmie, Co-Founder at ForeverLawn, Inc.**

DEDICATION

To Zaden and Zaiden

Zaden, thank you for believing in me and seeing me as a masterpiece. Without you, this book would not exist.

Zaiden, my son, you were named after a man who believed in people more than they believed in themselves. I co-dedicate this book to you and ask you to believe.

Table of Contents

ACKNOWLEDGMENTS

Brittany, where would I be without you? You are patient during the late nights of writing and world-changing. You are beautiful beyond compare.

To my family—thank you for your ongoing support and loving encouragement.

The MLS team: Bill, Bobby, Ronda, Ry, Erin, Heather, Laurie, Karen, Mike, and Brittany. I appreciate your service towards helping people live fulfilled and impactful lives.

To Mark Lamoncha, Bob Bertelsen, Dale Karmie, Brian Karmie, Dave Hughes, John Dilling, Rob Mehno, Troy Radinsky, Don Mook, Lance Hostetler, Lynda Dickson, Valerie Mayer, Rich Bereschik, Linda Rolley, Dave Buzzard, Kent Polen, Tom Cunningham, Kevin Ours, Bill Lish, Paul Daniels, Austin Berryman, Bob Bast, Tim Bast, Steve Crumblish, Doren Wengerd, Conrad Troyer, Matt and Michele Horn, Steve Sochacki and many more...

Thank you for allowing me to serve your organizations with this message. You are all tremendous leaders!

Forward
by Brittany Ross

Our self-image is quite possibly the most crucial aspect of living a fulfilling and impactful life. When our self-image is broken, we live a life of brokenness. When our self-image is healthy, we live a life of power, purpose and passion.

In *A Clear View*, Michael B. Ross imparts value to his readers, teaching them that within each person is limitless potential for healthy, whole, and meaningful lives. He provides practical tools for tearing down negative belief systems and developing the thought patterns necessary to build a positive self-image.

As Michael's wife, I've watched firsthand how Michael has worked through the very processes he's written about. Both Michael and I have had broken places in our lives, largely brought on by a lack of self-acceptance and self-respect. Consequently, we've walked through some very dark experiences. Painful as those times were, they've given us the privilege of seeing restoration at work—in our own lives and the lives of each other. It's out of these very experiences that Michael's passion for helping others was born.

This book is a product of life experience, learning, and implementing what's been learned in order to break out of bad habits and into a life of peace. The stories Michael shares are relatable and the tools given for change are simple, yet profound. This book has the power to become a beacon of hope and a catalyst for lasting change. Read it. Use it. Be changed by it. You are worth every effort to become your best—and it all starts with a clear view.

Introduction

I'm going to speak from my heart for a moment.

I'm tired of people getting beat down by negative self-image. I'm tired of seeing millions of people not using their potential because they don't believe in themselves. I'm tired of the shortage of confidence I see in beautiful, talented, and inspiring people. I'm tired of hearing the stories of people afraid to take risks because they're worried about what others think. Negative self-image has kept so many people locked in self-doubt, self-hatred, and self-pity that they can't see the masterpiece they are. Enough is enough.

This book is about action. I've spent 15 years fighting negative self-image and although it still gets some hits on me from time to time, I have been whipping its tail consistently for a long time. The content in this book is a battle plan. It is all the practices I have learned from study, mentors, and experiences to help me defeat negative self-image. They are practices I still keep to this day.

This book does include some basic scientific information about how your brain works, why people have a hard time overcoming negative beliefs, and what we desire most as humans. However, the point of this book isn't to put you to sleep. The point of this book is to give you the tools you need to have a positive self-image, which in-turn, will lead you towards a fulfilled and impactful life.

If you're like me and you're tired of negative self-image getting the better of others or yourself, then join me in this fight. Together we can help the world get a clear view.

CHAPTER #1
My Self-Image

I was 11 years old. I was 4 feet 10 inches. I was a chubby 190 pounds. I had glasses and long greasy hair. Until that summer, I didn't really know how I looked to others. My dad had recently changed careers and my family moved to a new city for the second time in two years. My brother and sisters were really good at making friends and quickly did so after we moved. As the baby of the family, I lived in the shadow of my siblings. For a while, I tried riding my brother's coattails and begged him to let me hang around him and his friends. Although I'll never fully understand, there must be something extremely uncool about having your little brother hang around you and your friends. My brother was better than most. He let me follow him around at times, and other times he graciously turned me down. But, it was time for me to make my own friends.

My parents met a nice family who had a son named Darryl. That summer, Darryl was going to a camp for two weeks and many kids from area schools would be attending. My parents told me about the camp and introduced me to Darryl. I liked him immediately and decided I wanted to go to camp with him.

In the weeks leading up to camp, I dreamed about all the friends I would make and the popularity I'd have. I imagined walking through the camp giving high fives, back slaps, and big smiles to all my new friends. Also, I dreamed about meeting a girl. I was officially out of the "cooties" stage and into the "try-to-show-girls-I'm-cool" stage. One of my missions for camp was to meet a girl I could call my girlfriend.

After weeks of dreaming, the day of camp finally arrived. Scores of young men and women were dropped off by their parents. You could see the reluctant relief on parent's faces. They seemed reluctant to leave their middle-school-aged children in the care of camp counselors, but looked relieved to have 2 weeks of peace and quiet. After we said our goodbyes, we were directed to the camp's main building for check-in. As Darryl and I were waiting in line, the strangest thing happened to me. My palms began to sweat, my heart began to race, and logical thoughts escaped me. There, in the girls' line I saw the most beautiful girl I'd ever laid eyes on—a girl with perfect hair, eyes, and face. I felt like one of those cartoons where the characters heart beats out of their chest. I looked at Darryl and said, "Dude, I've gotta talk to her!" I didn't have a plan. I didn't have rhyme or reason. I just knew I had to talk to her.

We dropped our stuff off in our room, and then I began surveying the camp for this girl. After looking for what seemed to be an eternity, I finally spotted her. She was standing by a swing set talking to her friend. Again, my palms began to sweat. Never before had I been so nervous to talk to a girl. For at least those moments in time, this was the only girl in the world. I thought long and hard (well, at least 10 minutes) about a strategy for approaching her when a plan crystallized. Darryl and I would walk up to these girls and I would strike up a conversation by saying something extremely cool and witty. I believed the girls would be overwhelmed by our charm and good looks, guaranteeing they would want to hang out with us for the rest of the camp.

I told Darryl about my plan and he didn't seem overly excited. It was almost like he didn't believe it would work. But, as good friends do, he agreed to stand by my side. As we approached the girls, butterflies were swirling around my stomach, and my forehead began to perspire. Fear was cropping its ugly head. I contemplated turning back. I wanted to retreat, but I trudged ahead like a warrior in battle and spoke to her.

Instead of saying something charming and witty, I said something completely dorky like, "So, do you like to swing? I could push you."

Fail.

I didn't know it at the time, but girls have radars that go off when a guy shows interest in them. She was obviously a seasoned professional at flirting and I was a rookie. Instead of graciously letting me down, she gave me no hope. She blankly turned to me and said, "You're fat and ugly. I just wanted you to know that."

Game over.

Hurt? Disappointed? Embarrassed? No. Those aren't strong enough words to describe how I felt, more like devastated, hopeless, and crushed. It was bad enough she called me fat and ugly, but she did it with complete assuredness. She didn't follow with, "I'm just kidding" or, "I didn't mean that." She simply went back to her conversation as if I no longer existed. As if I was a plague and her words were the cure. I spent the next few weeks looking in the mirror chastising myself for being fat and ugly. The phrase, "You're fat and ugly" played through my mind like a song on repeat. Those words imbedded themselves deep into my subconscious.

Unfortunately, that wasn't the end.

A month after camp, another word sunk its teeth into my self-image: stupid. Since my family moved to a new county, we were required to take placement tests at the county educational offices. The day we went to take the tests, I had a baseball game and testing was the last thing on my mind. Every circle I filled in reminded me of a baseball I would hit. The lady giving the tests was blank and unfeeling, much like the pretty girl by the swing set. After testing was over and scores were generated, the lady brought my mom, my brother and sisters, and me into a conference room. She praised my brother and sisters for their high intelligence. She made special note of my brother who was well advanced for his age. I quickly realized I was the only one she wasn't praising. I optimistically thought, "Maybe she's saving the best for last." In that case, however, she saved the bad news for last.

In front of my mom and siblings, she talked about my poor test scores followed by her diagnosis that I had a learning disability. She was using really big words to explain my condition. As an 11-year-old, all I heard was, "blah blah blah, Michael's stupid." My mom is the sweetest lady in the world, but when she disagrees with something, she does so adamantly. She began to strongly disagree with the lady and they eventually had to agree to disagree. On the way home, my mom tried to reassure me I was smart like my brother and sisters. I appreciated her attempts to make me feel better, but I was smart enough to know there aren't many mothers out there who would admit their kids are stupid. The damage had already been done.

Fat. Ugly. Stupid.

Those three words became the wardens in my prison of self-hatred. I was deeply wounded but I didn't want to admit it. I didn't want to admit I was weak. I didn't want to admit people's words had control over me. Instead, I began to hate my image. I hated who I was perceived to be. I hated who I was. I hated my future. In addition, I began to hate the world around me. I hated rules. I hated regulations. I hated school. I hated organizations. Most of all, I hated people. I hated how I didn't feel good enough. I hated how people can be so cruel even in the face of kindness. I hated how people are selfish. I especially hated the fact that in spite of my hatred, I longed to be accepted and loved.

I was hurting. But instead of working through the pain, I decided to get even. The words from Timon of *The Lion King* resonated with me. "When the world turns its back on you, you turn your back on the world." The words fat, ugly, and stupid were lies I told myself over and over and over again. And the more I believed those lies, the more bitter, angry, and malicious I became.

The eight years following my 11-year-old summer, my self-hatred grew. I got into tons of fights, lied all the time, I stole from friends and family, I cheated my way through school, I treated girls like pieces of meat, I vandalized property, I manipulated good people. I did all kinds of drugs, I drank a lot, I burned, punched, and cut myself, and I cut others with words. I thought by hurting others I could make my hurt disappear, but it only made it worse. Behind my "tough guy" persona was the 11-year-old boy wounded by the words, "fat, ugly, and stupid." Those words beat me into a dark corner and held me there.

I believed I was no good so my actions were no good. Eventually, my behavior led me to a jail cell. I vividly remember sitting in a cell with 15 other guys while waiting to see a judge. The men in the holding cell weren't shy about sharing who they were and the time they had done. One guy talked about doing time with his dad. He was almost proud of it. Honestly, I felt sorry for him. If anyone deserved an excuse it was him. His dad set an example for him and he followed. Simple as that. Me? I had no excuses. My parents raised me right and I turned away.

Like most others who have been through hurt, I had no idea I allowed my past sufferings to dictate the man I had become. All I knew was men were supposed to be tough and showing pain is a sign of weakness. I thought by suppressing the hurt it would go away, but it was in the darkness that it grew. Metaphorically, the hurt became infected and eventually became a disease. It controlled me.

The judge was candid. He simply looked at me and said, "Son, I've seen your case a hundred times. I suggest you join the military or get into a service organization. If you don't, you'll wind up behind bars for a long time." His words resonated. One thing about unresolved hurt is it makes you extremely selfish, sensitive, and defensive. I had spent so much time trying to protect myself from getting hurt again, I'd not given any thought to helping others. So when the judge mentioned service as a way of avoiding imprisonment, I became intrigued.

Soon after my meeting with the judge, I was on a flight heading to boot camp.

In boot camp, I met another recruit named Zaden. Besides my parents, I never met anyone who could look through me and see who I was under my hurt, bitterness, and hardened exterior. Zaden saw me not for who I was, but for who I could become. Day after day he would tell me things like, "Michael, there's something special about you. I just can't put my finger on it." Or, "You're going to do something special with your life, I can tell." He would talk to me about how he overcame hurt and rejection in his life. His story was compelling and I began to believe if change was possible for him, perhaps it was for me.

One night I told Zaden my story. It was the first time I'd ever admitted being hurt by people. He allowed me to air my dirty laundry, he allowed me to talk negatively about people, but he didn't judge me. After I was finished he simply said, "Michael, your story is going to end in a masterpiece." He wasn't just giving me a line—he truly meant it. He believed in me when I didn't believe in myself. He gave me hope when I had none. He gave me a fresh perspective on who I could become.

A few days later I had a one-sided confrontation with my drill instructor. Apparently, he had recognized negative behavior in me and he wasn't going to take the soft approach. He gave it to me straight. "Ross," he said. "I've been watching you. You're a real punk, you know that? I want you to look at your shirt, pants, and boots." I obeyed. "I want you to look at the man on your left and your right." I did. Then he got right in my face and said, "They've got the same shirt, pants, boots, and haircut as you. You're not special! What makes you special is what you do for that man on your left and man on your right."

Suddenly, everything Zaden had told me began to make sense.

I realized making your life a masterpiece isn't about making your life interesting so people will marvel at your greatness, it's about living your life beautifully so others will see the beauty in themselves.

For years I had focused on myself. I realized making your life a masterpiece isn't about making your life interesting so people will marvel at your greatness, it's about living your life beautifully so others will see the beauty in themselves. I finally understood that everything in life is about serving others. Once I knew and understood that, I knew it was time to change.

It was time to become someone who could get a clear view of myself in the mirror without insults, chastisement, and fear. It was time to change my self-image.

CHAPTER #2
Your Self-Image

In order to develop a positive self-image, I had to be honest about my story. Before you can change, you have to understand your own pain. So what's your story? We all have one. That is, unless, you've lived on an island by yourself your entire life. But even that's a story. Who hasn't been hurt, disappointed, or rejected? Pain is a fact of life. The question isn't whether or not you've had pain, but what have you done with it? If you're

The question isn't whether or not you've had pain, but what have you done with it?

anything like I was, you've tried to bury it. You may have put your pain in a metaphoric closet hoping it will never be opened. You also may have formed negative habits in order to mask it. Nonetheless, you've had pain. Most people never work through their pain; they walk around wounded and never experience the power of a positive self-image.

We all struggle with maintaining a positive self-image. It's so easy to see the flaws in others. It's easy to find the speck of dirt in other's eyes. Sometimes it is hard to take a hard look at ourselves and admit we have flaws, weaknesses, and struggles. Other times, it is hard to see our strengths. Developing and maintaining a positive self-image isn't easy, but it is worth it because every step, every obstacle we overcome, and every person we touch makes a monumental difference in our lives and in society.

Think about it this way: What if you broke your arm in an accident and you decided that instead of going to the hospital, you were just going to pretend you're not hurt. You wanted to "tough it out" and "suck it up" and deal with the pain. You think to yourself, "Eventually it will heal" and "I'll be fine." However, the pain remains. Every time you shake someone's hand, pick up a pen, or start your car, the pain reminds you of your accident. But, you keep trudging along pretending you're ok. Without realizing it, you begin avoiding people for fear of having to shake their hand, you avoid writing for fear of picking up a pen, and you avoid driving for fear of starting a car. Pretty soon you're isolated, living in fear, and masking your pain.

This scenario seems ludicrous, doesn't it? If we had a broken arm, most of us would head straight to the hospital, get it set, casted, and take medicine for the pain. After it healed we would go through physical therapy and get it back in shape. Right?

However, when it comes to internal brokenness we avoid healing at all costs. We hide, mask, and isolate. Most people would rather die than face the pain of their past. Do we intend to avoid healing? No, most of us do it subconsciously, but nonetheless, we do it. As a result, the majority never lives up to their potential. They never develop and cultivate relationships or reach their career ambitions because of pain. Many of us never make a significant difference in the lives of others. Most people are walking around with a crippled self-image because the fear of pain has them locked into an internal dungeon.

Often people with poor self-image feel isolated. In reality, statistics show individuals with negative self-image are not alone:

- According to Dr. Joe Rubino, 85% of adults have a negative self-image.
- 97% of women say one negative thing about their bodies every day.
- 80% of men do not believe they have enough muscle definition.
- Negative self-image is a common denominator among nearly all addictions to mind altering substances.
- In a worldwide research study, the World Health Organization reported that more deaths are caused each year from suicide

than homicide or war.

- It is estimated that around 50 million Americans suffer from a diagnosable mental disorder in any given year.

- Negative self-image has been linked to violent behavior, school dropout rates, teenage pregnancy, and low academic achievement.

Ask yourself the following questions:

1. How would you describe yourself?

2. Are there any negative words you or someone else has used to describe you?

3. If so, do you believe that they are true?

4. Who is someone in your life who has encouraged you?

5. What positive traits do you think they see in you?

6. Overall, do you feel like you have a positive or negative self-image?

7. Can you think of any specific behaviors that resulted in a negative self-image?

Moving forward, you will be given tools to build a positive self-image. It's important for you to look inside yourself and determine where you may struggle. As the old saying goes, "To change the world, we must start with ourselves." Building a positive self-image is not easy. It will be a war. You must remain in every battle in order to win the war.

CHAPTER #3
Belief Creates Reality (or Unreality)

When Mandy was 3 years old, she fell down her stairs and her cheek was caught on a loose nail. Her momentum tore her cheek open. Her parents rushed her into a busy hospital where an on call doctor quickly gave her five stitches. Because the doctor rushed his suture, the wound took longer than normal to heal. When it did, it left a noticeable scar. Month after month following the accident people would ask, "What happened to Mandy's cheek?" Kids who played with her often asked what happened. Over time the scar faded and it became less and less noticeable, but not to her. When looking in the mirror, Mandy would stare at her scar. She hated it. She thought about it numerous times a day. Instead of working through the pain, however, she started to hide.

She learned how to hide her blemish when interacting with others. In middle school, she grew her bangs long to cover half of her face. Mandy longed for friendship and attention from young men, but she shied away for fear she would be rejected because of her scar. The scar didn't just affect her physiology; it affected her psychology, her personality, and her relationships. Because she spent so much time focusing on her scar, she believed that's all others focused on as well.

Mandy went to college to be a social worker. Her desire was to help others who suffered with physical and emotional scars. She believed if she could help others overcome their pain, perhaps she would heal in the process. In college, Mandy made a close friend–alcohol. Drinking numbed her pain and helped her throw off inhibitions. While drinking, she was able to ignore her pain. However, when she wasn't drinking, it would overcome her again. Mandy liked who she was when she was drinking. She was fun, free, and friendly. Alcohol helped her stop caring what people thought. At first, she only drank on the weekends, but soon she began drinking on the weeknights as well. Then, she started drinking at all hours of the day. Anytime she would start to come down, she looked for a drink. Because of her high intelligence, she was still able to get through college and graduate with honors.

After college, Mandy got a job working for a non-profit organization as a caseworker for troubled youth. One of her first assignments was to speak to a suicidal girl named Tasha. Tasha was born with a cleft lip. Tasha constantly called herself "an ugly freak" and "a waste of life." Mandy instantly identified with Tasha and had compassion for her. Mandy knew it was her responsibility to help Tasha, but if she couldn't help herself, how could she help someone else. Meeting Tasha pushed Mandy to find a healthy way to deal with her own pain and stop believing the lies she had been telling herself. Through her own healing, Mandy was able to help Tasha change her beliefs too.

In some ways, we're all Mandy. We all have scars. However, most of our scars aren't on the outside. We've all been hurt, maybe not by a physical object, but by people's words. We have all been made to feel foolish and have been gossiped about. We've all had people ignore us, ostracize us, and reject us. We've all felt like we want to hide and have created a negative behavior to help us mask our pain. It may not be alcohol, but it could be one of the many addictions such as; food, work, prescription pills, shopping, gambling, tobacco, or video games. Most of us don't know what to do with the pain of our present or past. Because we simply learn to cope, many of us live unfulfilled lives.

An unfulfilled life happens when fear keeps someone from living their potential. People fear failure, they fear exposure, they fear rejection, they fear humiliation, they fear themselves, and they fear not knowing if they really can. They tell themselves, "If I give it all I have and don't succeed, then what?" For some, hope without effort is better than effort without hope. Perhaps the most debilitating fear is the fear of success.

An unfulfilled life happens when fear keeps someone from living their potential.

Ask yourself these questions: Are there things in your life you want to do but aren't doing? Is there something inside you telling you that you can overcome any obstacle life puts in front of you? Do you feel there is something great inside you that's longing to be unleashed? Then ask this: What are you afraid of? Perhaps your own greatness scares you more than pain, failure, or rejection.

Take a look at this poem by Marianne Williamson:

Our Deepest Fear:

Our deepest fear is not that we are inadequate.

Our deepest fear is that we are powerful beyond measure.

It is our light, not our darkness that most frightens us.

We ask ourselves, "Who am I to be brilliant, gorgeous, talented, fabulous?"

Actually, who are you not to be? You are a child of God. Your playing small does not serve the world.

There is nothing enlightened about shrinking so that other people won't feel insecure around you.

We are all meant to shine, as children do.

We were born to make manifest the glory of God that is within us.

It's not just in some of us; it's in everyone.

And as we let our own light shine, we unconsciously give other people permission to do the same.

As we are liberated from our own fear, our presence automatically liberates others.

I believe that deep inside we all know this poem is true. As a life and business coach, I have talked to many people over the years who allow fear to keep them from taking risks, building relationships (including their families), and doing things they have always wanted to do. Fear keeps them from changing into the person they want to be. Deep down we should all believe we are meant to do something great. So, how do we go from the desire to change to actually changing?

CHAPTER #4

The Path of Belief

When I was a young man, a group of friends and I decided to blaze a new trail in the woods and build a tree fort. So, we gathered wood, found machetes and hatchets, and made a new path in the woods. We found a cozy spot to build our tree fort and began construction. After a couple weeks, it was finished. At first, our trail was hard to find, but the more we walked on it, the easier it was to see. Eventually, we walked the path subconsciously, without thinking about it.

Years later after returning from the military, I was reminiscing about my childhood and decided to go see the old fort. I drove to the woods and looked for the old path, but two things had happened. First, I couldn't remember where the path began. Second, the weeds had grown back because no one had walked on the path in years. After looking for awhile, I found a different entrance to our old fort. Much to my chagrin, someone had torn down our fort and the wood was lying on the ground, covered by moss and leaves.

Our mind pathways are very similar to paths in the woods. The more we go down certain paths, the easier it is for us to go on them again. In fact, we go down most pathways without thinking. Our mental pathways form our beliefs about ourselves, and then we reinforce those beliefs by our actions. As Albert Wolters once said, "Either your actions will change to fit your beliefs or your beliefs will change to fit your actions."

Whatever you believe about yourself, you follow with action. When you attempt to act outside of your normal behavior, either your actions are stifled by old beliefs, or new beliefs will be created. If you believe you are worthless and that nothing you do matters, you may not be living up to your full

Whatever you believe about yourself, you follow with action.

potential. You may not be living a healthy lifestyle, expanding your knowledge, or sharing your gifts with others. When you take a different course of action, you can create new beliefs about yourself.

Belief in yourself is vital. Faith, trust, assurance, and confidence in who we are and our abilities give us the strength we need to overcome life's obstacles. Have you noticed those who believe in themselves achieve the most? Muhammed Ali once said, "It's the repetition of affirmations that leads one to belief. And once that belief becomes a deep conviction, things begin to happen."

You can succeed if others do not believe in you, but you cannot succeed if you do not believe in yourself. Many people throughout history overcame poor self-image. Martin Luther King Jr. was a dominant force in the civil rights movement during a time that most said equality was impossible. Michael Jordan's high school basketball coach cut him from the team. Much of society told our American forefathers they had zero chance at gaining independence. Over a dozen publishers turned down J.K. Rowling's Harry Potter series before a British company finally purchased it. Roger Banister ran a four-minute mile after experts said for years it was impossible. Each of these men and women proved someone wrong. By believing in themselves and their causes, they helped other people to change as well.

Now imagine if each of these men and women would have agreed with their naysayers. What would have happened if our forefathers didn't write the Declaration of Independence? What if Michael Jordan quit playing basketball or Martin Luther King Jr. didn't fight for equality? Life as we know it would be different. Without a strong belief in ourselves, we will not succeed and we will not be able to serve the world with our unique gifts, talents, and abilities.

CHAPTER #5

The Greatest Belief of a Negative Self-Image

We could spend a lot of time talking about symptoms of our pain, or we could get to the root of it all. The greatest belief of a negative self-image is—you're not good enough. Think about this for a moment. Isn't your negative self-talk the result of you not feeling good enough? Have you ever used any of these phrases while talking to yourself?

"I'm stupid."

"I'm such an idiot!"

"I can't do that."

"They're so lucky. I'm so unlucky."

"I wish someone would notice me."

"If only my boss/teacher would recognize me."

"If only I was more attractive he/she would want to be with me."

"I'm not worth the effort."

"I'm too...(negative word)."

"Why do bad things always happen to me?"

These and thousands of other phrases exemplify negative self-talk. Though each phrase seems to manifest itself differently, the root belief remains the same: I'm not good enough. For example, "I'm stupid," is a way of saying, "I'm not good enough." "I can't do that," is another way of saying, "I'm not good enough." "I'm so unlucky," is saying, "I'm not good enough." It is vital to recognize the root of the issue so we don't treat the symptoms. Unless we have fought through the difficulties of over-coming the beliefs at the core of negative self-talk and accept our true value, then we will continue to struggle with not feeling good enough.

Where you are in life is the result of your choices, whether they've been good, bad, or indifferent decisions. A great error in judgment is to assign a person value based on the decisions they've made to that point. It's easy to say a drug dealer is a "waste of life" and to say a teacher, city councilman, or a generous business owner is "a good person." Then if a drug dealer turns his life around, it's easy to sit back and say, "Well, he was once a bad person and now he's a good person." We tend to place value on people based on their actions and not the inherit value they have as a human being. The problem with this philosophy is we then attach our own personal value to our performance or to others' opinions of our performance in life. If we are "performing" well, or others think we are "performing" well, we feel good about ourselves. This keeps us in a place of constantly striving to feel good about ourselves, or perpetually hiding so that others don't see our flaws.

When I do training on character in organizations, I like to start with a game called lifeboat. The game starts with this scenario: 15 people are on a boat that is sinking. There are no rafts, floating apparatuses, or any other life saving device which people can use to stay afloat. The only thing that is available is a lifeboat that holds nine people. If more than nine people get into the boat, it will sink and everyone will drown. Each person participating in the game is given a role to play. They are as follows:

PREGNANT WOMAN	PREJUDICE EXTREMIST
THERAPIST	DRUG DEALER
USED CAR SALESMAN	PRIEST
EX-CONVICT	PROFESSIONAL ATHLETE
MALE NURSE	BILLIONAIRE STOCK TRADER
FEMALE PHYSICIAN	ANGRY 18 YEAR OLD FEMALE
NEWS ANCHOR	7 YEAR OLD BOY
POLITICAL LEADER	

After roles are given, people give a short argument on why they believe they should have a spot on the lifeboat. Once arguments are given, the group determines who gets on the lifeboat and who is left out to sea. Take a moment and put a check mark next to the people you would save on the list above.

Nearly every time I've facilitated this game, the people who are left out to sea are the used car salesman, the ex-convict, the political leader, the prejudice extremist, the drug dealer, and the professional athlete. Why is that? Because in our minds, whether we like it or not, we determine a person's value based on what they do. In addition to that, we are especially quick to determine a person's value if we benefit or are hurt by their actions. If someone helps us in a time of need, we determine him or her to be a good person. If someone rips us off, we consider him or her a bad person. Most of the time, however, these determinations are made subconsciously, but in reality a person's value is not based on what they do.

You are valuable beyond measure.

You are valuable beyond measure. No one, including yourself, could put a price tag on the value of your life. Your life is worth more than the greatest sum of money, the greatest treasure, and the most elaborate experience you could have. You are the most brilliant, most elaborate, and greatest sum to ever walk the earth.

There is an ancient saying, "Greater love has no one more than this: to lay one's life down for one's friend." The reason this statement is powerful is because only another life is equal to the life of another. Only true love in us recognizes the value of our life and the life of another. In order to live with true love we must stop attaching the value of our lives to the value of our choices.

Your choices do not determine your value as a person. Your choices hinge upon the value you've given yourself. They are not one and the same. Ask yourself the following questions:

- Would a person who values himself or herself choose to stick a needle in their arm and pump their veins full of heroin?

- Would a person who values himself or herself choose prostitution as their profession?

- Would a person who values himself or herself cut themselves with razors?

- Would a person who values himself or herself not take good care of their health?

- Would a person who values himself or herself cheat on an exam or tell lies to get ahead?

- Would a person who values himself or herself intentionally devalue others with their actions and words?

- Would a person who values himself or herself treat others with disrespect?

- Would a person who values himself or herself not take care of their finances?

- Would a person who values himself or herself not take time to read, study, or increase their knowledge?

"You is kind. You is smart. You is important." This line, from the instant classic movie *The Help*, describes each of us in three short sentences. You are kind when you give of your gifts, talents, and abilities to the world. You are smart when you find your strengths and work in them. You are important to your family, friends, and the world around you. Your actions don't make you kind, smart, and important. However, your actions do reveal the level of kindness, intelligence, and value you place in yourself. Your gifts belong to you and you alone. The greater value you give yourself the greater effectiveness your gifts will have. Your self-image is your greatest champion and your worst enemy. As Jim Rohn used to say, "To do more in life, you must become more." In order to heighten achievement, inspire others, and live a fulfilled and impactful life, you must value yourself. You must start chiseling away your negative self-image.

The following was written by my beautiful wife, Brittany:

Michelangelo is arguably the most talented artist of all time. From his work at the Sistine Chapel to his gorgeous depiction of "The Creation of Adam," his masterpieces have wowed art enthusiasts and laymen alike for centuries. Perhaps his most famous work is a statue called "David." The 17-foot tall statue represents Michelangelo's artistic expression of one of the Bible's most heroic and inspiring characters: King David.

When Michelangelo was asked how he made this breathtaking statue, it's reported he said, "It's easy. You just chip away the stone that doesn't look like David." With the kind of vision that can only be understood by a true artist, Michelangelo saw David within an oversized, banged up, and damaged slab of marble. His work began with an image. He saw David before David could be seen by others. With his chisel he patiently and methodically chipped away every part that wasn't David until a masterpiece emerged.

Michelangelo's work was painstaking. It wasn't easy and it wasn't instantly gratifying. He pressed on with determination.

An ancient teacher told his students, "You are a masterpiece, created for a special work." Every one of us is a masterpiece inside. We all have something special to offer the world. We all have something inside of us that's dying to be unleashed. However, it takes long-suffering and determination to bring out our masterpiece. We must start by staring our negative beliefs in the eyes and telling them, "You have come far enough and today you go no further."

Make no mistake, you will never overcome negative self-image unless you admit you've not valued yourself and accept and believe the true value of who you are. Your belief in your true value is the most important way to achieve a positive self-image. Once you are willing to accept and believe you are valuable beyond measure and you are worth the effort of having a fulfilled and impactful life, then everything will change for you. You will like the changes.

Never forget, your value is not based on your actions. Your negative self-talk creates a path towards negative behavior. Pain creates lies that we tell ourselves which leads to negative self-talk and negative behaviors. In order to gain a positive self-image, you have to stop telling yourself the lies and change the behavior.

CHAPTER #6

Change, Belief, and the Power of Words

Change is simple. Jim Rohn said, "Change is about picking a new destination and going that way." When you decide you are going to have a positive self-image, you simply need to go there. As I stated earlier, the starting point of a positive self-image is your belief in yourself, others, and life's possibilities. Belief is the acceptance by the mind that something is true. When you start to believe you are good enough, your actions will follow and allow you to share your gifts with the world.

Belief is the acceptance by the mind that something is true.

Human beings learn in two ways: First, through repetitive auditory and visual stimulations. Second, through intense emotional experiences. What we say, hear, think, see, and discuss on a regular basis is reinforced by what we do. As we repeat sights, sounds, and actions, we form our beliefs about the world, including ourselves. To change our beliefs, we must start by changing our repetitive communication patterns. In short, we must change our self-talk. Anthony Robbins once said, "The quality of your life is the quality of your communication." We must confront the words we use, how we use them, and then pick a new communication destination and begin going that way. Words are powerful.

Words are like a machete in our brain paths; they clear the way towards a specific destination. They have the ability to heal and the ability to tear down. Words can remind us of our value or cover it. The following song "Words" by Hawk Nelson gives a great description of the power of words:

They've made me feel like a prisoner

They've made me feel set free

They've made me feel like a criminal

Made me feel like a king

They've lifted my heart

To places I'd never been

And they've dragged me down

Back to where I began

Words can build you up

Words can break you down

Start a fire in your heart or

Put it out

Words create our world. Just think about the difference between "can't" and "can." Can't shuts doors, can opens doors. Can't limits influence, can expands influence. Can't crushes self-belief, can energizes self-belief. Can't confines action, can increases action. Can't decreases creativity, can is creative. Just the difference in one word creates a completely different world.

King David once said, "The word is a lamp to my feet and a light for my path." Words are like lights to guide us through the darkness in our life. For example, have you ever been confused about something and someone came along and used carefully chosen words to help you understand? The words they used are like guiding lights. Their words helped you see the path. On the other hand, words can cast shadows on the light in our life. Have you also had someone attempt to explain something and they confused you even more? The words they used were like shadows. Their words darkened your path.

It is so important to understand the power of words when it comes to our self-image. The average person speaks at a rate of 120-150 words per minute. However, people think at a rate of 1,000-1,500 words per minute. We are constantly speaking to ourselves. In fact, you are having one or multiple conversations with yourself right now. You may be thinking of something you need to do later, you may be thinking about a personal relationship that's facing challenges, you may be thinking of something great or silly you've done, so forth and so on. You are constantly speaking with yourself. If you're not mindful of your thoughts, you may be forging a self-debilitating path.

CHECK POINT

Now that we've covered the basic causes of a negative self-image, it is time to overcome. In the following pages, you will be given the tools needed to defeat self-debilitating beliefs and unleash the power of a positive self-image. Changes won't occur in an instant—it's a daily process. But be encouraged, "Anything worth having is worth working hard for." The story of Michelangelo in the previous chapter is a great example of what's needed in order to unleash the power of a positive self-image. The word character means the image on a coin that is hammered out by a chisel. As we start to believe in our own worth and value, our decisions hammer away at the things in our lives that don't belong. There will be days when you feel like quitting. There will be days when you question if you're making any difference at all. There will be days when you face resistance from seemingly everyone in your life. Let me say this ahead of time—it's ok. What's important is to keep hammering away. The power of a positive self-image will be unleashed in time and the world will marvel at the masterpiece that's revealed. You are worth it!

Step One

Defeating and Replacing
Negative Self-Talk

CHAPTER #7
Form New Beliefs and Defeat Negative Self-Talk

The first step towards unleashing a positive self-image is defeating negative self-talk. This practice will take discipline. It will be laborious, tedious, and at times, altogether painful. As the ancient saying goes, "No discipline seems pleasant at the time, but painful; later on, however, it produces a harvest of good living and peace for all who are trained by it." The first three months of fighting negative self-talk will be a stretch, but it will afford you great momentum which is the key to sustaining success in self-talk.

To defeat negative self-talk, take the next three months to engage in these three practices: track your thoughts, challenge your thoughts, and replace negative self-talk.

TRACK YOUR THOUGHTS
Find a way to track negative thoughts by using a journal, writing on a notepad, or whatever method works the best. Note things like how you are feeling, the people you are with, your environment, or the weather.

> Example A
> While in the department store with a friend I saw an outfit I would like to purchase. I instantly thought I would look bad in the outfit.

> Example B
> While at an event with a few of my classmates a negative/sarcastic comment was made about a project I am working on. I instantly began to think I was a failure and started condemning myself for not being good enough.

> Example C
> While at school, a group of students began laughing about

something and I assumed they were laughing at me. I then began thinking about all of my negative qualities and by the end of class, I was feeling depressed.

The point of tracking isn't to go into vast detail. The purpose is to turn the volume up on your thoughts and determine why you're thinking the way you are. You can then evaluate the validity of your thoughts. In addition to tracking the negative thoughts about yourself, track the negative thoughts you have of others. Often times, the negative thoughts we have about others reflect the negative thoughts we have of ourselves.

At the end of each day or week, take time to look at your tracking system and see if you find consistent patterns. Do the thoughts come when you're with a particular group of people? Do the thoughts come in a particular environment? Are the comments focused on a specific aspect of your character? Are the comments focused on your physical appearance? Is there a particular word or phrase which triggers your negative self-talk? Ask these questions and more to divulge the nature of your thoughts. At the end of each week, examine your tracking system and determine if there is a pattern to your thoughts. Examples of consistencies might be your environment, people you are with, your physical appearance, particular words or phrases that acted as triggers, or a specific aspect of your character.

CHALLENGE YOUR THOUGHTS
Earl Shoaff said, "Stand watch at the door of your mind." Our minds are like thought factories and we are the plant managers. The thoughts we allow in our factory will show up in the production of our lives. In order to have the type of production which will lead us to a fulfilled and impactful life, we must challenge the negative thoughts which come into our minds. Remember this short saying, "What you think, is what you feel, is what you do." The following steps will help you challenge your thoughts.

Determine if what you are thinking is true. According to studies, people lie to themselves multiple times per day. Many of the lies are subconscious. During any day, you may begin to feel depressed, discouraged, or ashamed without knowing why. When this happens, it is very important to get some time by yourself and turn the volume up on your thoughts. What you may discover is you are thinking and accepting lies about yourself. We are much more likely to accept lies we think about ourselves than lies we are told from others.

After you turn the volume up on your thoughts, try to determine what thoughts are there. Next, say the thoughts you're thinking out loud and ask the question, "Is this thought true?" Separate the thoughts you believe are true from the thoughts you think are lies. Enlist the help of a trusted friend who will be truly honest with you and hold you accountable as you move forward.

Focus on the thoughts that you have identified as lies. Determine where these thoughts come from. Just as a tree's roots are buried deep in the ground, lies have their roots under the surface in our lives. Once you have discovered and challenged the lies in your life, it is then time to unpack the lies and kill the root. To get to the root of your lies, it is important to get some time alone and meditate on your past. Psychologists have shown when you are looking for mental clarity on any subject, that 22 minutes of uninterrupted silence is the average time it takes for a person to be in a state of clear thinking. As you are trying to discover the root of your lies, do not sell yourself short. Take the proper time to get to the root.

A great phrase to remember with any process of self-discovery is, "Don't just think it—ink it." Make sure you are writing down your thoughts and reading them out loud. This creates a 3rd party perspective which will allow you to see yourself from an outsider's viewpoint. A few questions to ask while doing this exercise is: When do I first remember hearing this lie about myself? Who was the first person who told me this lie? How old was I when I first remember agreeing with this lie? How often do I agree with this lie? How have I reinforced this lie with actions?

Once you have unpacked the lies, it is important to write the lies out in a simple phrase. A few simple examples: I'm not good enough. I'm worthless. I'm stupid. I can't ever live up to their expectations. I'm not as good as they are etc. Remember, words create our world. If you aren't clear in identifying the words you use against yourself, it will be difficult to counteract them. Be disciplined in writing them down and saying them out loud so you can recognize the root lies when other words or phrases infiltrate your mind.

REPLACE NEGATIVE SELF-TALK
After you have taken the proper time to challenge and unpack the lies you have settled with, it is time to replace the thoughts. It is much easier to redirect energy than it is to shut it down. Consider this: most of your thoughts are habits. Mahatma Ghandi said, "Your thoughts become your words. Your words become your actions. Your actions become your habits." If you are going to change negative self-talk, you are going to have to form new habits with your thoughts, words, and actions.

Many people try to quit habits "cold turkey" through willpower to no avail. I can speak about this from experience. Years ago I was a smoker. When I first tried to break the habit, I threw a half pack of cigarettes in the garbage and vowed I would never smoke again. Then, just three hours later, I was digging through my trashcan to find the pack of cigarettes so I could smoke. If you're laughing and thinking, "I've done something similar to that," then you know the power habits can have over our lives.

The trashcan incident taught me that in order to change, I'd have to change my thinking. At the time I thought I couldn't live without cigarettes. My thoughts needed to change about cigarettes, so I decided to replace cigarettes with chewing tobacco. It was one bad habit for another. But, I quit smoking. Goal achieved! Unfortunately, chewing tobacco was much more difficult to quit. I eventually replaced chewing tobacco with pouches and replaced pouches with chewing gum. Now, many years later, the thought of smoking or chewing rarely crosses my mind. Please know that I'm not recommending that a person replace one bad habit with another. I simply want you to know that replacing habits is much easier than quitting something cold turkey. Try replacing your bad habit with a good habit. Replace negative self-talk with positive self-talk!

CHAPTER #8

Choose Positivity over Negativity

Mother Teresa was one of the most loving, generous, and compassionate people who ever lived. She served the poorest of the poor without asking for anything in return. Unfortunately, Mother Teresa did not go without scrutiny and adversity. She was criticized for some of her views, the media doubted her motives, and people of the Christian faith questioned some of her relationships. Nonetheless, she stayed true to her mission of serving people. People thought criticism didn't bother her, that she was immune to negativity. But in her memoirs, Mother Teresa wrote about the pain and frustration people's negative comments caused her.

Yet, she made a choice that no matter what people said about her, she would continue to do what she felt was right. She used the following poem to help her stay positive. It is called the Paradoxical Commandments:

People are often unreasonable, irrational, and self-centered.

Forgive them anyway.

If you are kind, people may accuse you of selfish, ulterior motives.

Be kind anyway.

If you are successful, you will win some unfaithful friends and some genuine enemies.

Succeed anyway.

If you are honest and sincere people may deceive you.

Be honest and sincere anyway.

What you spend years creating, others could destroy overnight.

Create anyway.

If you find serenity and happiness, some may be jealous.

Be happy anyway.

The good you do today, will often be forgotten.

Do good anyway.

Give the best you have, and it will never be enough.

Give your best anyway.

In the final analysis, it is between you and God.

It was never between you and them anyway.

So much truth resonates from this poem. Most of the greatest achievers have made a choice to think positively in the face of negativity. When you make a choice to develop and maintain a positive self-image, negativity will come. It will come from multiple sources. Perhaps you come from a family who is negative who may influence you to be negative. Maybe you're working in a profession you don't enjoy and it brings you down. Or it could be that you've been so used to sabotaging yourself when you make changes, that your negative self-talk becomes more aggressive when you try to take a better path. Regardless of the source, you will face negativity. You must be prepared to make a paradoxical choice. This process is simple (notice I didn't say easy, I said simple). You must decide to choose positive over negative.

NEGATIVE PHRASES AND SAMPLE REPLACEMENTS
Phrase: I'm not good enough
Replacement: I'm worth it

Phrase: I'm (any of the following: fat, ugly, a degenerate, a dirt bag, etc.)

Replacement: I'm a masterpiece

Phrase: Nobody cares about me
Replacement: Somebody needs me

Phrase: Life sucks and then we die
Replacement: Life is great

Phrase: I hate (any person, place, thing, or idea)
Replacement: I appreciate (any person, place, thing, or idea)

Emotion is one of the most powerful forces in the world. However, our feelings aren't always based on the truth. There have been so many times I've spoken to an individual or a crowd about replacing negative self-talk and someone asks, "If I say those things but don't really feel that way, doesn't that make me fake?" Let me in turn ask a question—is truth true? For example, does one plus one equal two? If you answered yes, then we agree on that truth. If I were to walk around saying, "I feel like one plus one equals three" and I believed it and told myself, "one plus one equals three" over and over again, would it change the truth? Would the truth change for me? Absolutely not! Truth doesn't change, truth is real. It is reality.

When we consistently act upon truth, we become free people who live beautifully.

Therefore, if you agree with a feeling based on a lie about yourself or others and you act upon that feeling because you don't want to be "fake," then you—in fact—become fake. Truth is real regardless of how you feel. Saying, thinking, and doing the right thing must be done in the face of our feelings at times. When we consistently act upon truth, we become free people who live beautifully.

The truth is you are a masterpiece. You are worth it, life is great, someone needs you, and there are many things in life to appreciate. Make the paradoxical choice to believe truth over lies. Begin using your self-talk to affirm the truth about yourself rather than the lies. When the people in your life drag you down with negativity, combat their influence with the power of positive self-talk. Remember, you can succeed if no one believes in you. You can't succeed if you don't believe in yourself. Believe in yourself and use your self-talk to reaffirm and solidify that belief, regardless of what the world around you projects upon your life and your choices.

CHAPTER #9

Get Connected

Getting and staying connected is invaluable to defeating and replacing negative self-talk. Why? People are built for relationships. Studies show that people with healthy relational connections achieve more goals, are happier, have less grief, fewer bouts of depression, and better immune systems. Connection in relationships with other human beings is an essential building block to a positive self-image. When people struggle with negative self-talk, their tendency is to isolate themselves from people or hide who they truly are in front of people. Social isolation causes negative self-talk to have greater influence. When negative self-talk has greater influence, people are much more susceptible to anxiety, depression, fear, and doubt. My dad has a great quote, "Relationships are the bridges over which values are transferred." Developing a deep relationship where you can share your values as well as your struggles will offer you great benefits. It will keep you from social isolation, allow you to have a partner in challenging self-talk, and give you more fullness in life.

Connection in relationships with other human beings is an essential building block to a positive self-image.

COMMUNICATION: THE LOST ART IN CONNECTION

I recently received an email from a successful businessman who told me he has thousands of acquaintances and connections through social media, but no friends. We have become so "connected" through technology that we've become less skilled in communication. Social media, texting, and other electronic communication methods are great, but they were meant to be a supplement for enriching relationships, not a replacement for interpersonal communication. As much as I enjoy when someone "likes" or comments on my posts, it is not a deep connection to that person. Deep connections can only happen through face-to-face or voice-to-voice communication. Here is why:

NON-VERBAL COMMUNICATION

Fifty-five percent of communication is non-verbal. When you're face-to-face with someone, you are able to read their body language, facial expressions, eye movement, hand gestures, and head placement. Your body language communicates if you're happy, sad, confused, scared, relaxed, stressed, playful, silly, angry, etc. When you eliminate non-verbal cues from communication, you miss much of what is not being said, which emphasizes what is spoken.

COMMUNICATION THROUGH TONE OF VOICE

Thirty-eight percent of communication is tone of voice. My mom used to say, "It's not what you say, but how you say it that makes the biggest difference." After years of studying human communication, I realized she's right. We can say the same phrase in hundreds of different ways. By your tone you can offend or uplift a person. You can be sarcastic or whiny. You can be friendly or arrogant. When you eliminate tone from communication, you entrust the reader of the message to correctly interpret your intended tone.

COMMUNICATION THROUGH WORDS

Seven percent of communication is words. This is why it is so difficult to write a great article, paper, or book (and if you've ever read academic writing, you know how boring reading can be). It takes a skillful writer to draw the reader towards common expression, tone, and emotion.

Most people are using written words to communicate the bulk of their emotions to a great portion of their relationships. Unfortunately, most people are not skilled writers. I mean none of this with disrespect. I simply want to offer an explanation for why people are feeling disconnected. I also want to implore you to make real connection, with people. Don't just text—call. Don't just Skype—meet at a physical location. Spend time with people who you share common interests with. Think about what you are passionate about and explore ways to meet other people around those passions. If you exercise, then join a gym or take a class to meet people. If you like art, take an art class and connect with others. There are websites and groups dedicated to helping people connect around common interests. Statistics show that people have fewer true friends now than they did 20 years ago. I believe this is the result of greater communication with fewer connections. To have greater connection in relationships in the 21st century, you will need to be intentional about putting down the cell phone, shutting the computer, and turning off the tablet to start getting shoulder-to-shoulder with people—not just their pictures and videos on social media.

CHAPTER #10
Love And Acceptance

Once you've made connections, it is up to you to become vulnerable and open in your relationships. It is also important to constantly evaluate your relationships because again, your self-image is greatly affected by your relationships. If you're surrounded by people who make you feel important, build you up when you're feeling down, and encourage you to be the best you can be, it will nourish a positive self-image in you. If, however, you're surrounded by people who intentionally or unintentionally make you feel foolish, worry about their needs above everyone else, and don't push you to be the best you can be, your self-image will lean towards the negative. We will be like those we hang around. As the ancient proverb says, "If you hang with the wise you become wise, but a companion of fools suffers harm."

Aristotle said, "In poverty and other misfortunes in life, a true friend is a sure refuge." The deep need we have for connection comes down to our need to be loved and accepted. Never forget these two important facts about people:

The number one desire of a human being is the desire to feel important.

The number one fear of a human being is the fear of looking foolish.

As a human being, you are important. No matter what anyone has told you, regardless of what you've believed about yourself, you deserve to be loved and accepted for who you are. In addition to that, you are worth having relationships which will nourish, strengthen, and lead you towards a positive self-image. Do not settle for less than the best just because you may be comfortable hanging around people with whom you are familiar. Get out of your comfort zone. Connect with new people. You may be surprised what kind of relationships you can have when you search for something better.

Life is too short to journey alone.

Life is too short to journey alone. Be intentional about communicating face-to-face and developing deep connections with people who will nourish your self-image. You deserve the best!

CHAPTER #11

Develop Toughness

I've been known to be a bit competitive. Ok, that may be an understatement. I grew up with an older brother, Christian, who had a goal to make me tough. He did this by beating me in every facet of life. He beat me intellectually by getting better grades, he beat me physically when we fought, and he beat me in sports. I specifically remember playing him one-on-one in basketball and he wouldn't let me score. If we played to 11, his mission was to beat me 11-0. If we played to 7, he wanted to beat me 7-0, so forth and so on. There were times when I would cry and he would tell me to quit whining and keep trying. There were times I would get so frustrated I'd sucker punch him and he'd beat me up, pick me up, and tell me to try again. Our competitions were infinitely one sided. But, as my Pap—Bob Tatgenhorst—used to say, "Either you can keep getting beat, or you can do something about it." I decided to do something about it.

I began to work on my skills and physical ability when Christian wasn't around. Regardless of the sport or game, I wanted to improve so I could beat him. I practiced non-stop. If I wasn't practicing basketball, I was practicing Nintendo. If I wasn't practicing Nintendo, I was practicing baseball. You name it; if we competed in it, I practiced. As a result, I began winning. I'll never forget the first time I beat him one-on-one in basketball. I was 16 years old and Christian was home from college. We went to the court where we'd played as kids and I beat him—over and over. He was in disbelief because he was so used to beating me and frustrated about losing because he couldn't do anything to stop me. After I won for the fourth time, he finally turned from his frustration and he began to compliment me on getting better. The feeling of satisfaction was like nothing I'd ever experienced.

Christian achieved his goal of making me tough. He did it by making me earn every point I scored against him. He never took it easy on me. He never allowed me to wallow in self-pity. He congratulated me when I won.

As you develop a positive self-image, negative self-talk will not let up. Negative self-talk will keep you scoreless as long as it can and will beat you as often as it can. It will never surrender. Unlike my brother Christian, negative self-talk will not defeat you for a positive purpose; it seeks to beat you down and keep you down. Additionally, it will never congratulate you when you win. In fact, negative self-talk will try to steal your thunder. It only has one purpose—to keep you from living a fulfilled and impactful life. Therefore, you have to develop toughness to keep negative self-talk from penetrating your self-image.

Toughness is the resistance to breaking under repeated twisting and bending forces. Toughness is developed through fire. In our fast-paced, have-it-your-way culture, we have lost an element of toughness. We have enjoyed great affluence because of the hard work of those who have increased our economic standing, military protection, and relationships with other nations. However, affluence can be negative if people rest on the hard work of those who came before them and don't take their hard work to the next level.

As Sir Isaac Newton said, "If I have seen further it is by standing on the shoulders of giants." It is the responsibility of a generation to make the ceiling of the previous generation their floor. As the ancient proverb says, "Without vision, people stop caring." When people rest on the laurels of those before them, they begin to value comfort over character, and as I said in my book, *Overcoming the Character Deficit*, when you value comfort over character, you get neither. Toughness requires getting out of your comfort zone and walking through fire. It requires you to "get tough" in your battle against negative self-talk in order to improve upon greatness in our generation. We

Toughness requires getting out of your comfort zone and walking through fire.

must develop the toughness it takes to solidify a positive self-image and disarm the power of negativity in our lives. All who have made a significant impact in this life have faced opposition—negative self-talk is your opposition and it must be defeated in order to move on into a life of wholeness and positive impact. Do not make a choice to let negative self-talk define you. Instead, recognize it for what it is and replace the lies you tell yourself with the truth. You are a masterpiece.

CHAPTER #12
Setting Goals

T.E. Lawrence said, "Those who dream by night in the dusty recesses of their minds wake in the day to find that all was vanity; but the dreamers of the day are dangerous men, for they may act their dream with open eyes, and make it possible." Dreamers of the day are goal-setters. To have a positive self-image, you must be intentional. Setting goals is intentionally saying you are ready to take action. This sets you up for adversity, and adversity is the fire that develops toughness. Setting goals towards a positive self-image is daring negative self-image to stop you— this is inevitable. You cannot avoid fire if you are going to achieve your goals. All people face adversity, but tough people welcome adversity and walk right through it. Goals will enable you to keep your purpose in mind as the heat of adversity begins to rise.

SET BIG GOALS
The B.I.G method will enable you to set meaningful goals that will lead you along the path of developing a positive self-image. Here is a simple way to set self-image goals using the B.I.G. method:

> **B – Believable.** Your goals need to be something you look at and think, "I can do that." You don't want to set goals that could overwhelm you, but you also don't want to sell yourself short.

> **I – Inspiring.** Your goals should inspire you both in the short and long term. You should be able to look at your goals daily and have instant motivation to achieve them.

> **G – Grand.** Your goals need to be bigger than solely your wants, needs, or desires. If you are the only benefactor from your goals, it is easy to lose motivation over an extended period.

Examples of good and bad goals:

Bad – I will never say a negative word about myself.
Although this is commendable, if you have been speaking negatively to yourself for 10, 20, or 30 years, the chances of you changing this habit overnight is slim to none. A goal like this is not believable and this could easily burn you out.

Good – I will develop positive self-talk by challenging negative self-talk so I can be an inspiration to my family and friends.
This goal is clear about what you want (positive self-talk), what you need to do (challenge negative self-talk), and why you're doing it (to be an inspiration to family and friends). This is a B.I.G goal. It's believable that you can develop positive self-talk, it's inspiring to challenge negative self-talk, and it's great to want to develop positive self-talk so you can help others.

This is just one example of many. Be sure to set one goal at a time to avoid burnout. The process of developing positive self-talk is one step at a time. Don't rush it.

WHEN YOU GET KNOCKED DOWN—GET BACK UP
Setting goals is like having a scoreboard for your life. If you're working towards your goals, you're winning, and if you aren't working towards your goals, you're losing. My brother Christian says, "Your will to win must overcome your fear of failure." Many people do not set goals because they allow their fear of failure to overcome their will to win. This thought process is ludicrous because there isn't a person alive who has ever batted 1,000, made every sale, had a perfect marriage, received 100% on every test, or known how to solve every problem. Everyone in life gets knocked down. The difference between winners and losers is slight. When winners get knocked down striving for their goals, they get back up, losers don't. Winners believe in themselves even when the odds are stacked against them, losers stop believing. Winners work harder when they lose in order to correct their mistakes, losers make excuses. The difference in action is slight, but the outcome is

monumental.

One of the greatest speeches I've ever heard about winning versus losing came from the movie *Rocky Balboa* when Rocky's son is blaming Rocky for his lack of personal success. Rocky responds like this:

> Let me tell you something you already know. The world ain't all sunshine and rainbows. It is a very mean and nasty place and it will beat you to your knees and keep you there permanently if you let it. You, me, or nobody is gonna hit as hard as life. But it ain't how hard you're hit; it's about how hard you can get hit, and keep moving forward. How much you can take, and keep moving forward. That's how winning is done. Now, if you know what you're worth, then go out and get what you're worth. But you gotta be willing to take the hit, and not pointing fingers saying you ain't where you are because of him, or her, or anybody. Cowards do that and that ain't you. You're better than that!

CHANGE OF PERSPECTIVE

One thing we have to do when it comes to winning and losing is change our perspective. We should define success in terms of taking action instead of just win or lose. Why? As long as we take action, we are successful in achieving results. If you are playing baseball and you swing three times, miss three times, and strike out, you are achieving a result. The good news is, if it's not the result you want, you can go back and correct what you did wrong and try again. The only way you ever lose in life is if you stop trying. As one coach used to tell me, "You will miss 100% of the shots you don't take."

The only way you ever lose in life is if you stop trying.

CHECK POINT

Before Zaden told me I was a masterpiece, I had little belief in myself. I began to see how genuine he was and how much he believed in me, so I started to believe in myself. Once I believed I had value beyond measure, I began to confront my negative beliefs. I tracked my thoughts, I used positive words instead of negative words, I built strong life-giving relationships, and I developed toughness. None of it was easy. I didn't write this book to sugarcoat things for you.

Building a positive self-image is difficult and will require a lot of work. The most difficult part of the task is defeating and replacing negative self-talk. It forces you to look inside yourself and to confront many of the negative beliefs you've told yourself. It forces you to look back at painful experiences from your past. It requires taking the time necessary to heal from those painful experiences. This will take vigilance. You will need support, you will need discipline, and you will need love. I know the "hard-work and discipline" talk may not be what you want to hear, but as George Washington said, "I cannot tell a lie."

However you shouldn't do the hard work and discipline for me or anyone else. Do it because you have infinite value. You are worth every effort it takes to have a positive self-image, which leads to a fulfilled and impactful life. Defeat negative self-talk, beat it into submission, make it cower before you, and then drive it out of your life. I believe in you. You are a masterpiece!

Step Two

Build Confidence

CHAPTER #13
What is Confidence

Years ago while teaching a group of high school students, I asked that all students who struggle with confidence raise their hands. Every student raised their hand, except one young man. He (we'll call him Andre) was a good-looking, star football player, an academic achiever, and very popular. To my shame, in the back of my mind, I thought Andre was probably masking narcissism for confidence, so I asked him a question. "Andre, tell us what gives you confidence." He looked me straight in the eyes and without hesitation he said, "Well, I'm a hard worker. I'm nice to people. And if I tell someone I'm going to do something, I do it." I was a bit taken back by his answer. It was one of the most mature answers I'd ever heard from a high school student. In the eyes of most of his peers, he was a high school student who had it all. Surely he felt confident from his many achievements and not from his character, right? Wrong. He did not put his trust in his appearance, achievements, or social status. Instead he stood on the principles of character.

Confidence comes from the Latin word *confidere* which means to have full trust in. When we have confidence in something, we believe it is strong and will stand in the face of opposition. However, confidence can be fragile depending on what we have confidence in. For example, let's say each day on your commute to work you drive over a particular bridge. Day after day and year after year you drive over the bridge without questioning its strength or integrity. You never consciously think to yourself, "Should I trust this bridge?" You have full confidence that the bridge will stand under the weight of your vehicle. Now, let's say one day as you drive over the bridge it begins to shake and wobble. You barely make it to the other side and when you look back you see the bridge's pillars shaking. What would you do the next time you drive to work? Would you chance going over the bridge or would you take a different route? To have a positive self-image, we must be confident that the bridges in our lives will hold up over time.

CONFIDENCE VERSUS SELF-CONFIDENCE
I struggle with the term self-confidence. Having self-confidence implies that a person has full trust in oneself. Numerous self-confidence teachings instruct people to rely on themselves for everything in order to be successful. However, many people I've coached who have bought into that ideal have been left with a worse self-image then when they started.

Why? Humans are fallible. We make mistakes. We break promises we make with ourselves. We intend to say one thing and do another. We are like the unsteady bridge. Therefore, having self-confidence or self-trust is a bit of a misnomer. We must instead trust in what isn't fallible, what doesn't break promises, and what will always be steady. A proverb says, "He who trusts in himself is a fool; but those who walk in wisdom is kept safe." We must have confidence in the unchanging principles of character. Again, character means the mark or stamp on a coin which is hammered out by a chisel. Each time we put confidence in character we increase our self-image because we are relying on something that will never let us down.

CONFIDENCE IN CHARACTER FOR A POSITIVE SELF-IMAGE
Character provides an unshakable foundation for a positive self-image. Examples of character principles are:

Ambition	Justice
Boldness	Kindness
Consideration	Loyalty
Dependability	Optimism
Encouragement	Passion
Friendliness	Responsibility
Generosity	Selflessness
Honesty	Teachability
Imagination	Compassion
	Wisdom

Each of these character traits is firm, solid, and true. Could you imagine someone blaming honesty for their lack of success? What if someone came to you and said, "If it wasn't for responsibility, I'd be much further along in my life."

This seems outlandish, but many people do not trust character because of bad experiences. I recently had a student tell me character doesn't work because the last time she showed kindness, the other person treated her poorly. So, I asked if she believed being unkind would help her achieve her goals. She said no. I asked if rudeness would help her get a job. She said no. I asked if disrespect would help her make friends. She said no. The student had every right to feel hurt from being treated poorly. However, just because someone reacts negatively to character doesn't mean character doesn't work. One foundation of character is accepting that we control our actions and reactions and no one else's. Character works if people work character. Unfortunately, not everyone applies positive character traits to their life. That is a fact we need to accept before moving forward. For those who do work character, however, they can expect a positive self-image with unshakable confidence.

Building confidence through character is a journey best accomplished one step at a time. Three character traits that will help build your confidence are teachability, honesty, and courage. As we move

Character works if people work character.

forward, you will understand the connection between these three character traits and how they will impact your confidence. Begin by working on one of these three traits, after you have worked on each trait individually, go back to the trait you started with. In his book *Outliers*, Malcolm Gladwell said mastery comes after you have spent 10,000 hours practicing a skill. Character is a skill you must practice. With practice over time, you will become a master. Let's become masters together!

CHAPTER #14

Teachability

Perry was a very smart young man. He had the ability to figure things out through observation. Pete was smart, but often needed help learning new things. Because Perry knew he was smart, he didn't listen to the advice of others. Pete, on the other hand, valued the advice of others because he wanted to be the best at whatever he did.

Perry and Pete started playing baseball in second grade. At first, Perry excelled because of his ability to observe and apply what he learned. Pete didn't do as well at first, but gladly accepted the advice of his coaches and other teammates and practiced what they taught him. As they moved to the upper divisions, Pete kept improving while Perry started to struggle. Coaches and teammates offered Perry advice, but he was unwilling to listen. Sometimes he'd even do the opposite of what they were telling him because he wanted to be sure he could do everything on his own.

When they reached high school, Pete was far better than Perry. He listened to advice and accepted instruction. Perry distained advice and rejected instruction. The coaches saw that Perry had talent, but decided to cut him from the team. They wanted players who were willing to listen and grow. Pete is now playing baseball in college on a scholarship and continues to improve, and Perry has not played since middle school. What was the difference in these two outcomes? Pete was teachable and Perry was not.

WHAT IS TEACHABILITY
Teachability means the willingness to learn by being taught. Brian Tracy says the two most common characteristics of successful people are 1) continual and veracious learning and 2) practicing what they learn. Every confident person I know is constantly learning. They read books, attend seminars, take classes, ask really good questions, and listen well.

Confident people don't worry about not knowing something because they know they can find answers. Unconfident people lie about what they know or don't know out of the fear of looking foolish. When they do this, they limit their success, because what we learn is what we practice. The following practices will improve your teachability.

Confident people don't worry about not knowing something because they know they can find answers.

KNOW YOURSELF

Socrates said, "The unexamined life is not worth living." He adamantly instructed his students to know themselves in every area of life. Knowing yourself takes hard work, intense contemplation, and discipline. Therefore, you must remain committed to learning more about yourself, even when you think you know everything about yourself. Socrates also said, "True knowledge exists in knowing that you know nothing." In short, you must learn, learn, and learn some more.

Ways to increase your self-knowledge:

- **Take personality profile tests**
  Get online and take personality profile tests. If you would like to take extensive tests, you can find some at a minimal cost. There are also many free tests you can take which will offer you in-depth explanation of your personality type. Many also explain how your personality affects your tendencies, habits, and interpersonal relationships. Take as many tests as you can and examine the results.

- **Ask someone you love and trust**
  Sit down with someone you love and trust and ask them to give you an honest evaluation. Ask them to describe your greatest strengths and weaknesses. Ask them what they see as a great career for you. Ask them to evaluate you as a father, mother,

friend, sibling, co-worker, or boss. If you can have a list of questions for them before you meet, it will help them prepare their answers. To increase your self-knowledge, you should remain objective and refrain from becoming defensive. Some of the things your confidant will tell you may hurt, but if you remain objective, the information they share with you could catapult your knowledge of yourself.

* **Write a timeline of significant events from your life**
Take a sheet of paper and write a line horizontally. Think back to your childhood and write the date of significant events, both good and bad, from your life. Examples could include: Hit my first home run, made friends with (name), family vacation, mom and dad divorced, or graduated high school. You should write anything you consider significant, even if others would question what you write down. After you write the timeline, get a separate sheet of paper and write how each event affected your view of yourself.

* **Journal**
Christina Baldwin said, "Journaling is a voyage to the interior." Journaling allows you to precisely see how you are feeling and thinking about past, present, and future. You should carry a journal with you almost everywhere you go. Journaling will help you gain clarity if you are pondering an important decision, but it also gives you a great opportunity to write down your creative ideas. Additionally, carrying a journal will increase your learning from others. If you hear a great quote or idea, you can jot it down in your journal. One great quote or idea can be the spark that lights up our lives.

Most importantly, by journaling you begin to see yourself from a third party perspective. You'll begin to build a relationship with yourself like you've never had before. Ultimately, the better you know yourself, the better decisions you will make. For example, if I discover through journaling that I'm an easy sell and I'm trying to save money, then I will better prepare myself if I'm put in a situation where someone is trying to sell me something.

- **Admit your strengths and weaknesses**
Psychologist Roy Baumgardner says that 87% of people are overconfident in their abilities. A major reason people are overconfident is they aren't honest with themselves. Many people are comfortable talking about their strengths, but are afraid to admit weaknesses. Admitting weakness will give you freedom. Knowing your strengths gives you clarity on how you should spend your time, talents, and effort. Knowing your weaknesses will allow you to lean on others or to seek people who can help you improve. For example, if you're a salesperson and you're not particularly good at writing proposals, you can hire someone to help you. Or if you are struggling in math, you can find a tutor. An ancient proverb says, "Our strengths are made perfect in weakness." Think about this proverb for a moment. If you were to delegate your weaknesses to others who are strong in that area, you are perfecting your weakness. Additionally, you will be more effective in your strengths because you will have fewer weaknesses hindering your progress.

Once you begin to know yourself, you will be able to appreciate who you are and that will build confidence. This will also help you make better decisions. For example you might be less likely to make rash commitments. How often do you say "yes" without knowing whether or not you'll be effective in your commitment? Over-committing in areas that aren't our strengths works against our efforts to build confidence. Take the time to learn about yourself and it will lead you towards better decisions and a positive self-image.

INCREASE YOUR KNOWLEDGE
An ancient proverb says, "The wise store up knowledge, but the mouth of a fool invites ruin." Teachable people constantly learn new things. They see learning as an adventure into a world they've never seen or a

place they have never visited. Teachable people are able to gain knowledge from anyone or anything, if they take the time to listen and learn.

Ways to increase knowledge (Here are some ideas that you may want to try.):

- **Get "from" the day**
  How many times have you heard someone say, "I'm just trying to get through the day?" What an awful way to live. With that kind of narrow thinking a person could miss the opportunity to learn something that could change their life. Instead, we should follow the advice from the great Jim Rohn and try to get "from" the day. If we make it our mission to absorb everything we can from each day and not miss any chance to learn, we will learn at least one new lesson per day. Over a year, that's 365 lessons. Again, words create our world. Replace the phrase "get through the day" with "get from the day" and you'll be astounded with the results.

- **Read (at least) one book per month**
  A good friend of mine has a great saying when he's feeling out of sorts. He says, "I need to increase my word count." What he means is he needs to read more. When we read material that is increasing our knowledge, we are tapping into new parts of our brain. An average non-fiction book is around 25,000 to 50,000 words. If you read at least one book per month, you will have increased your word count by 600,000 words per year. Studies have shown the difference between those who make over six figures in income and those who make less than the average median salary is the difference in the usage of 3,500 words. By reading more, you will have greater control over your language. Reading will increase your communication skills, as well as your effectiveness. All of these skills will ultimately increase your value to your organization and your quality of relationships. Don't neglect to read.

- **Listen to inspiring material**
  Zig Ziglar used to say each person should turn their automobile into a university. The average commute to work is 22 minutes, which is 44 minutes round trip. If a person would listen to educational material on their commute to and from work just two days per week, that would equal nearly six hours of learning per month. In five months, this would be equal to the learning time you would get from a college course. You can listen to podcasts, audio books, and even recorded college classes. If you invest two commutes per week to learning, you will exponentially increase your knowledge.

- **Take a class or get a certification**
  If you are a student already, the important thing for you is to make sure you are getting everything you can out of each class you're taking. I am a big fan of formal education. I have two masters degrees, am a certified life and business coach, and have begun work towards my Ph.D. The reason formal education and acquiring certifications is so valuable is that you are tested on what you are learning. Reading, studying, and listening to educational material is excellent, but testing ensures you have retained what you have learned. Testing challenges us to stretch ourselves and even cram knowledge in order to achieve a high mark. Put yourself in a situation where you will be tested and don't be afraid to fail.

- **Write about what you have learned**
  G.K. Chesterton said, "Reading makes a learned man, writing makes a precise man." Similar to testing, writing forces you to become precise in what you know. An old saying is "the devil is in the details." If you've ever painted, you understand how true this is. A couple years ago, my wife and I painted our living room. We used rollers and large paint brushes for the major portions of our walls, but we painted the door and window frames with small brushes to be precise. The results of the project were beautiful. The detail work took us much longer than the rest of

the room, but if we had used rollers around the edges, the project would have looked shoddy. Learning, especially about new topics, can be similar to using rollers on a wall. Writing is like using a smaller brush to fill in the details of what you have learned.

Increasing your knowledge will increase your confidence, but you must practice what you learn. It is the application of our education that makes the biggest difference in our world. As an apostle once said, "Don't simply listen to the word, do what it says. A person who listens to the word and doesn't do what it says is like a man who looks in the mirror and after he leaves, forgets what he looks like. He is double-minded, unstable in all he does." Put what you learn into practice and you will turn knowledge into understanding. Then, once you have practiced something long enough, you will gain wisdom.

STAY HUMBLE
It never ceases to amaze me how quickly people forget where they came from after they have success. The old phrase "I picked myself up by my bootstraps" really irritates me. Regardless of the blood, sweat, and tears a person has spilled to gain success, they have had help. Opportunities had to present themselves for them to get a break. People had to believe in their cause for them to move up. At minimum, someone had to teach them the character they needed to persevere. Humility is the modest view of one's own importance. Everyone is important. Everyone has unique gifts, talents, and abilities. However, without character, circumstances, or people, success is unattainable. Humility is a key aspect of teachability because only those who are humble put themselves in a position to learn—from others, from life and from character. When we lack humility, we lack the very thought-process that allows us to become a student of our own life; always learning, always growing.

Ways to remain humble:

- **Remember where you came from**
  As you grow in success and confidence, be sure to reflect on where you came from. Think about all of the time, effort, and

sacrifice it has taken to reach your station in life. Michelangelo said, "If people knew how hard it was to gain my mastery, they would not think it was so wonderful after all." In addition to keeping you humble, your history can serve as an inspiration to others who want to reach your level of success. Sharing your story with others allows you to serve others in their journey.

- **Go to the library**
  If you're struggling with feeling prideful, take a trip to a public library. Walk through the aisles and look at the all the books you haven't read and all the things you don't know. It is humbling. Open a few of the books and read a few paragraphs. Allow the atmosphere to inspire you towards learning. Think about what you could learn if you would read, study, and teach the information contained in the library. No matter how much you have learned, the library will remind you that there is so much more to learn.

- **Laugh out loud at your mistakes**
  John Maxwell once said, "Be sure to laugh at yourself because someone else already is." Some people take themselves way too seriously. Laughter brings levity to our lives like nothing else. Prideful people fancy themselves too important to laugh about mistakes. To prideful people, mistakes are to be corrected, not taken lightly. Humble people celebrate mistakes because they see mistakes as a sign of progress. Morihei Ueshiba said, "Failure is the key to success; each mistake teaches us something new." I'm not suggesting you don't correct your mistakes; I'm suggesting that you use mistakes to humbly remind yourself you're not perfect. Laughing is a better method than chastisement. Laughter allows us to remain joyful in our journey—there will always be more to learn, different areas to grow in, and ways we need to change. Laughing through these processes makes life far more enjoyable. Laughter truly is the best medicine.

- **Be a kid**
  One thing I love about my kids is that they give me permission to be a kid. When I play with my kids, I get to be a superhero, a knight, a prince, and sometimes "the bad guy." Kids use their imagination; they enjoy life, and believe the impossible is possible. Some people don't allow themselves to engage in child-like behavior because they believe it makes them look weak or foolish. Sincerely humble people do not base their actions on how they look to others, but on how their actions will create the greatest freedom for themselves and those around them. Laugh at yourself, but recognize that child-like behavior is not appropriate in every circumstance. This practice must be tempered. However, you must beware if you start acting more like Captain Hook instead of Peter Pan.

- **Change your expectations of others**
  I have spoken to countless people who have limited their happiness, production, and belief based on what others have or have not done. One of the many faces of pride is superiority. Prideful people have unrealistic expectations of others. They believe others should live up to their expectations even when others don't know what their expectations are. Humble people, on the other hand, place high expectations on themselves, but give others grace. By changing your expectations of others you focus on things you can control and don't allow others to control how you feel. This will give you the privilege of enjoying people without seeing them through a measuring rod. This isn't to say you should invest in relationships with people who are constantly destructive. You should respect yourself and others. Tell people what you are going to do (and not going to do), and do it, regardless of what other people do or don't do. Don't buy into the illusion that others control you or that you can control others. You are in charge of you and no one else. Releasing our expectations of others allows us to spend more energy controlling our own behavior rather than trying to control the behavior of others.

Confidence through character begins by having a teachable spirit. There are so many books we haven't read, people we haven't met, experiences we haven't shared, and lessons we haven't learned. When we remain teachable, we invite wisdom to teach us all it can. And it will. If we allow ourselves to learn, we will begin to get from the day, instead of getting through the day. We will learn more about ourselves and we will release others from our unrealistic expectations of them. Being teachable will give you a childlike attitude, allowing you to be vulnerable and free, which will in turn inspire others. As Aldous Huxley said, "Experience only teaches the teachable." Remind yourself daily to learn something new. In continual learning, you will experience a life of discovery, humility, and positive self-image.

CHAPTER #15

Honesty

Have you ever met a truly confident person who was not honest? I haven't. Honesty is living in a state of truthfulness. Truth provides a stable base for confidence because the truth is solid, perfect, and right. The truth sets us free. Have you ever been in a situation where you have told lies and then admitted it? How did you feel after you admitted it? Would free be a good description? Confident people live by the truth and they are free because they live without the fear, doubt, and instability that comes with lies. Remember, confidence is about having full trust in the principles you live by. Truth needs to be at the base of every conversation, decision, and relationship you have. I love what Winston Churchill said: "The truth is incontrovertible. Malice may attack it, ignorance may deride it, but in the end, there it is." Honesty is truth in action. The following practices will help you live an honest life.

Be honest with yourself
Sometimes the truth hurts and it is a natural human tendency to avoid pain. Therefore, we're not always honest with ourselves. So often people hide from problems hoping if they avoid them long enough they will go away. There are people who won't open bills because they don't want to see the truth. Some people resist asking questions for fear of the answer. Other people won't get on a scale or look in a mirror because they're afraid of what they will see. The truth won't stop being the truth just because we avoid it. We must take time to have an honest conversation with ourselves and speak the truth of where we are.

If you are not where you want to be physically, say it. Get on the scale and look in the mirror. If you have gotten behind on your bills, say it. Open your mail and write down a plan for getting caught up. If you're not making enough money, look for additional job opportunities. If you're afraid of asking a question for fear of the answer, ask it anyways. Within every struggle is opportunity. You truly cannot move forward from difficult circumstances without truth as your foundation.

Have frequent conversations with yourself and keep track of what is going on in your life. As you track, here are some questions that can help you have an honest conversation.

- Who am I?
- Where am I?
- Do I like where I am in life?
- Why or why not?
- What's wrong with my life?
- Where am I off track?
- How can I fix what's wrong with my life?
- Do I need to have a better environment, friends, or career?
- Who do I need to become to fix these problems?

Do not avoid honest conversations with yourself. Honesty begins with you.

Be authentic with others
Honest people are authentic. Authentic is being genuine and original, as opposed to being a fake or a reproduction. Many people pretend to be something they aren't because they fear that people will reject them for who they really are. We have all been taken advantage of, rejected, or hurt. Authentic people admit their pains, failures, and fears; they don't hide them in order to make themselves look better. Ask yourself these questions:

- What would happen if you said exactly how you feel around others?
- What would happen if you said, "I'm feeling fearful around you because of something that happened in my past" or "I can feel myself shutting down around you because of your strong

personality"?

- What if instead of avoiding people who make you feel uncomfortable, you actually address your feelings?

There are two things that would happen.

First, you would create an environment of authenticity. As you allow yourself to be vulnerable and you discuss your feelings of weakness, you give others permission to do the same. Vulnerability cultivates depth in relationships, but someone has to take the first step. Second, you will become more comfortable in your own skin. My friend Mark Lamoncha often says, "We are all broken pots needing fixed." By speaking the truth of how you're feeling to others, you can celebrate who you are, flaws and all, with those you choose to share your life with.

Your authenticity may cause others to feel uncomfortable around you, but that's because most people aren't authentic. Authentic people appreciate other authentic people. Inauthentic people feel uncomfortable because when faced with authenticity, their own inauthenticity is revealed. However, it is very important to consider the feelings of others while practicing authenticity. There is sometimes a fine line between authenticity and rudeness. I've heard people say, "Well, this is who I am and if you don't like it, forget you" in order to excuse their rudeness. True authenticity is covered with grace, mercy, and kindness. It doesn't flaunt itself in order to shame; it reveals itself as to invite others to join the party. Authenticity may make others feel uncomfortable, but rudeness makes people feel combative. It is most important that we discern the difference between the two. Be authentic with others and the truth of who you are will invite truth into your relationships.

True authenticity is covered with grace, mercy, and kindness.

Be authentic with your unique gifts

Stephan was preparing to move to another country and he bought a special gift for his friend Sheri. He was going to give the gift to Sheri at his farewell party the day before he was leaving, but Sheri came down with the flu and was not able to attend the party. So Stephen asked Carl, a mutual friend, to give the gift to Sheri the next time he saw her. He instructed Carl to make sure he gave this gift to her because it would help her tremendously. Carl agreed and asked what the gift was. When Stephen told him what it was, Carl was instantly filled with excitement for Sheri, but wished he had this special gift for himself.

When Carl went home that evening he began to deliberate over the gift. He reasoned, "Stephen will never know, all you have to do is give Sheri a counterfeit gift." After hours of contemplating, Carl decided to give Sheri a counterfeit and keep the real gift for himself. Years went by and Carl rarely used the gift, he hid it for fear that Stephen might come home on a whim and find out what he had done. Therefore, the gift went unused. Its radiance was never shared with the world.

What's the point?

It is so easy to read this story and to call Carl a liar, cheat, and thief. Indeed he did display those actions, but let's look at it from another angle. Gifts are meant to be given, shared, and used, they are not meant to be hidden. Everyone has been given unique gifts. Some of us have been given a gift of athleticism, musical talent, or leadership. Others have been given the gift to solve problems, create innovations, or teach. Still others have been given the gift of compassion, exhortation, or joy. And we have all been given the gift of life, relationships, and opportunity. Yet, how many people use their gifts, talents, and ability to make the world a better place? How many people practice and hone their gifting to share with others? How many people pass their knowledge and skills on to those who share their passion? I will give you the answer: Not many. Too few people overcome negative self-image and give the gifts they've been given. Therefore, without knowing, myriads of people are living like Carl, giving a counterfeit version of themselves to the world. They are not being authentic. When you don't freely share your gifts with the world, you are robbing people of you.

Ask yourself these questions:

- How do you know your gifts won't contribute to the cure for cancer?

- How do you know whether or not your gifts aren't going prevent people from committing suicide?

- How do you know your gifts won't create a new source of energy?

- How do you know your gifts won't be the inspiration someone needs to reveal their own gifting?

- How do you know your gifts won't create unity between nations?

The answer is we don't know. You have no way of knowing unless you openly give your gifts to the world without fear, doubt, or worry. Now, allow me to ask these questions in a more powerful way.

- What if your gifts revealed the cure for cancer?

- What if your gifts prevent people from committing suicide?

- What if your gifts create a new source of energy?

- What if your gifts will be the inspiration someone needs to reveal their own gifting?

- What if your gifts create unity between nations?

When we ask "What if?" we are asking if the effort is worth the reward. It is a question of value. If you give your gifts freely, there is a chance people will ridicule, reject, and ostracize you. There is a chance things will not work out the way you hope. There is also a chance you will have times of financial instability, times of doubt, and times of discouragement. Even so, the reward is greater than the risk. If you live a life of authenticity from the center of who you are, you will feel alive in ways you've never imagined. You will have experiences you've never dreamed of, and you will impact others' lives in ways you never thought possible.

The fight to become authentic is not about trying to make yourself something you're not. Think about it. Society has been trying to change you your entire life. Advertisements make you feel like you don't look good enough or you don't make enough money. People have told you you're not special or your ideas are stupid or you don't fit in. Circumstances may have limited your opportunities or made you believe you can't achieve your dreams. Therefore, you end up like a horse chasing a carrot on a stick or a hamster in a wheel, constantly striving to become someone you aren't in order to fit into a broken world. Becoming authentic is never about being someone you are not; it is about fighting to be who you really are. This is why knowing yourself, being vulnerable, and telling the truth is so important. Every time you do these things, it brushes back the lies you tell yourself. Fight to be who you really are; give freely of your unique gifts and don't rob the world of you. What if?

HOW LYING AFFECTS CONFIDENCE
A proverb says, "When you tell the truth, fairness is done, but lies lead to unfair treatment." If you have ever been treated unfairly then you know how important it is to tell the truth in every situation, because nobody wants to be treated unfairly as a result of someone else's lies. Pamela Meyer, the author of *Liespotting: Proven Techniques to Detect Deception*, says the average person lies 10 to 200 times per day. To be truth tellers, we need to be aware of common ways we lie so we can counteract the behavior when they arise. The following is from an article written by Dr. Lisa Firestone, titled "The Ways We Lie".

Controlling a response
When you talk to a close friend about an interaction with a co-worker or lover, do you only tell your side of the story? Do you leave out a small but significant detail about something you brought to the table? Do you rephrase the less desirable words you said in the moment? Think about how these subtle changes

may influence your friend's attitude and response. Are you just getting your friend to say what you want to hear? In the end, how authentic is their response if you strategically manipulated the outcome?

When you control a response by shading the truth, you create an alternate, agreed upon reality between you and another person. You then get advice that may be based on faulty information. Plus, you deny yourself the value and integrity that another person's true opinions might have awarded you.

Lying by omission

Have you ever complained to someone that you aren't losing weight without mentioning the Frappuccino you downed as an afternoon snack? Everyone has times when they leave out less-desirable details. Sometimes you do this to be sensitive or to spare a person's feelings, but sometimes those details matter, and you know it. For example, if your partner asks what you did that day, you may not mention that you wound up running into an ex and having lunch. Maybe you try to conceal an ongoing flirtation with a co-worker. These may not feel like acts of deception to you, but imagine how your partner would see them. Whether there's nothing to hide or something real you'd rather they not know about, leaving out significant facts will make you feel shady and creates a hotbed for further deceptions. On the other hand, creating an environment where you can be open about these things will promote a feeling of mutual trust and honest communication.

Exaggerations

People's insecurities about themselves may lead them to try to preserve a certain image of themselves, and they may experience a need for approval from others. However, when you exaggerate or don't represent yourself honestly, you are left feeling like a fraud, which further hurts your self-esteem. There's a fine line between highlighting your attributes and completely inflating your abilities. At work, you may promise to finish a task you know you won't be able to complete on time. You may exaggerate to a boss when it comes to your progress or skill level. Most likely, doing this will lead to trouble when your actions fail to match your words.

At times, you may lie to compensate for guilt. Parents often do this with their children, missing a soccer game, for instance, then promising they'll show up at every game for the rest of the season—only to disappoint again soon after. It's hard to hide a broken promise, a missed meeting, or a poor performance. Exaggerating deems you untrustworthy. Your words start to mean a lot less when the reality doesn't match up. Plus, you may never believe that you're being chosen or cared about for who you really are.

Self-Protection
Too often, people are coached by an inner critic to not express directly what they want or feel toward other people. You may have a guard up that tells you not to be too vulnerable. You may downplay your emotions or act like you don't care because you don't want to feel or look like a fool. But defending yourself with deceptions or false portrayals of who you are will drive you further from your goals and will likely prevent you from getting what you want in life.

Gossip or covert communication
Gossip is an epidemic. It's in every household, office space, and coffee house. It's a booming industry taking over our media. The biggest problem with talking about someone behind their back is that you may flat out deny these observations when face to face with that person. You can see how this can be harmful to your relationships. A true friend or loved one should be someone you can talk openly with, someone to whom you can offer feedback and welcome the same in return.

Another problem is that gossip breeds cynicism and destroys compassion. It's a nasty way of indirectly dealing with real observations or competitive feelings. When you favor direct communication over gossip, you become a more genuine, more compassionate, and not to mention, more appealing person to be around.

Lying can be overt or subtle. It is vitally important to know our lying tendencies so we can fight them. We cannot be authentic if we don't stand upon truth. If we're not authentic, we won't be confident, and if we don't build confidence, we can't have a positive self-image.

Truth is the price for confidence and a positive self-image. Be sure to take time to have honest conversations with yourself. Don't sugar coat things, tell yourself where you really are by using the questions from the chapter. Allow authenticity to reveal your unique gifting and to guide you into lifelong and fulfilling relationships. Above all, make sure you always tell the truth, the whole truth, and nothing but the truth. It will set you free.

CHAPTER #16
Courage

In 2002, after returning from the Middle-East to my duty station of Yokosuka, Japan, some friends convinced me to have a night on the town. We had just spent over 100 days in danger zones and they thought it would be a good idea to blow off some steam. Normally, when I went out on the town, I went as far away from base as possible because I had heard far too many stories of soldiers and sailors who drank too much, got into fights, and ended up in the brig (Navy jail). For some reason, I let my friends convince me to stay local and we set out for a good time. We ate at a really nice Japanese sushi restaurant, went to a massive arcade where we played games for hours, and then ended up at an American Country bar where there was supposed to be line-dancing. I had never been line-dancing before, so I thought I would give it a try.

We walked in the bar a little after midnight, there wasn't any line-dancing going on, so one of my friends went to the bar to find out when it would start. When he left, a guy about half my size said something smart to me. It was obvious he had been drinking by his saggy eyes and slurred speech. I hadn't had one drink and definitely didn't want to get into any kind of altercation, so I took the high road and said, "I'm sorry you feel that way" and went to find a place to sit down. Two of my friends and I sat down at a booth and waited for my other friend to return with news about line-dancing. Right after we sat down, WHAM, someone punched me in the back of my head. I looked up and it was the guy who smarted off to me when we first entered the bar.

Just to give you context, I had been working out with a few Navy Seals and EOD (Explosive Ordnance Disposal) guys and was in the best shape of my life at 6'3" and 215 pounds. The guy who hit me was maybe 5'10" and 150 pounds soaking wet. Anger swelled inside of me like a tidal wave as I thundered out of the booth and stared him straight in the eyes. He began jumping up and down like a prizefighter waiting for a bout. People were staring at us from all over the bar and fear came over me like a blanket. I wasn't afraid of fighting. When I was younger, I used to fight a lot and I would have begged for an opportunity like this. I was afraid of the ridicule I would receive if I didn't fight. As he was jumping around I put my hands in the air and said in a calm voice, "Listen bro, you don't want to do this and I don't want to do this. My friends and I just came out to have a good time; if I did something to offend you, I'm sorry," then I walked to the dance floor with my friends to wait for the line-dancing to begin.

A nagging voice in my head began to taunt me, "You sissy! You pansy! Everyone thinks you're a coward! Your friends are going to ridicule you and word is going to spread that you let that little punk push you around." I looked around the room and people seemed to be chuckling at me and the guy who hit me was laughing with the people he was with. My heart began to race and I thought to myself, "Maybe I should teach him a lesson. I mean, he hit me, I have every right to hit him back." As these thoughts were racing through my mind, the guy came up to me for the third time and began to egg me on. This time my friends tried to step in; I pulled two of them back and I looked at the guy and said, "We'll just leave. If there is anything I did, I apologize." As we were walking out, the guy and one of his friends were screaming curses at us, calling us cowards in the form of obscenities. Again the nagging voice in my head started, "You wuss! Just tell him to meet you outside somewhere. He came at you three times, he deserves whatever he gets." I wanted to follow the nagging voice, but a stronger voice in my head was telling me I was doing the right thing.

As we walked out of the bar, roughly 10 MPs (Military Police) were standing to the right of the entrance. Had I fought, they would've stormed into the bar and arrested us both. I would have spent at least three days in the brig, and at least 45 days on restriction and extra duty. Even after seeing the MPs, my humiliation was strong. I was struggling with feeling like a coward and feeling like I let the bad guy win. Additionally, my friends were talking about how they would've taught him a lesson and would never let anyone treat them like that. The walk back to base was long and silent for me. But when we got back to base, one of my friends said something to me I would never forget, "Ross, you're the strongest dude I know. As hard as that must have been, you did the right thing."

WHAT IS COURAGE?

The definition of courage is the ability to face danger, difficulty, uncertainty, or pain without being overcome by fear or being deflected from a chosen course of action. Courage is simply doing the right thing at the right time and in the right way. I used to believe courage was angrily looking fear in the face and trudging forward like a warrior, but I have learned you can be courageous while trembling in fear. As Nelson Mandela said, "I learned that courage was not the absence of fear, but the triumph over it. The brave man is not he who does not feel afraid, but he who conquers that fear." That night my internal desire was to beat that guy senseless. After reading the story, perhaps there's a part of you wishing I would have as well. I was trembling, not because I was afraid to fight, but because of what people might say if I didn't. However, the right thing doesn't stop being the right thing because of our feelings or fears. Had I fought him, I may have received some short-lived praise from my friends. I may have looked courageous, but I really would have been a coward because I would have succumbed to fear in order to avoid the humiliating consequences of doing what was right.

Courage creates confidence, which in turn creates a positive self-image. To be courageous we have to know what is right and then do it regardless of what is going on around us. We must know fear and how it affects each of us, and we must drive away influences that steer us towards making wrong choices seem right.

To be courageous we have to know what is right and then do it regardless of what is going on around us.

KNOW WHAT IS RIGHT
Take a few moments and think through the following questions. Simply answer the questions with either the term "right" or "wrong." Try not to over-analyze, just answer them based on your knowledge of the law and your personal convictions.

Questions #1

- In the United States of America, is it right or wrong to use marijuana?
- If you are on a sports team, is it right or wrong to quit when things get hard?
- Is it right or wrong to go to a party where you know people will be consuming illegal drugs?
- Is it right or wrong to talk negatively about your friends when they're not around?
- Is it right or wrong to steal food?

These questions seem like no-brainers, right? It probably took you less than a minute to go through this list and determine right and wrong. If only decisions were this simple. Life would be much easier if we could look at problems and quickly decide what to do without giving much thought. As you and I know; life isn't this easy. Life brings new situations every day and unless we properly discern right and wrong, we could end up on the wrong side of the ledger without knowing it. Now let's look at these situations from a different perspective.

Questions #2

- In the United States of America, is it right or wrong to use marijuana for a medicinal purpose?
- If someone is on a sports team, is it right or wrong to quit if they are being physically, mentally, and emotionally bullied by

other players and is on the verge of suicide?

- Is it right or wrong to go to a party to rescue a friend where you know people will be consuming illegal drugs?

- Is it right or wrong to talk negatively about your friends when they're not around if they are about to make a bad decision and you want to devise a plan to help them see the light?

- Is it right or wrong to steal food for your two-year-old sister who is starving?

I'm sure many of your answers changed from wrong to right. It is important to know people will judge you and others based upon what they believe is right and wrong. Unfortunately, many people judge before they get all the facts. They may see a person quit a team and quickly label them as a "quitter" without knowing the other players were bullying that person. People may judge a family for allowing their children to use marijuana before learning a doctor prescribed the drug as a treatment for their ongoing illness. People may judge someone for going to a party where illegal drugs are being consumed without knowing that the person went there to rescue a friend. This is why an ancient teacher told his students, "Do not judge others or you too will be judged; for the same measure you use to judge others will be used to judge you."

Why do I bring this up? Because whether we like it or not, people's judgments will influence our decisions. When you do the right thing, you will sometimes face scrutiny. We could talk all day about how people shouldn't judge, but we need to live in reality—people judge. Therefore, it is vigorously important for us to make sure we know what is good and right and true if we are going to live with courage. Each time we succumb to peer pressure and make a poor decision even though we know what is right, our self-image takes a hit. On the other hand, each time you make the right choice regardless of what others think, you build your confidence leading to a self-image.

HOW TO DETERMINE WHAT IS RIGHT

Know the laws of the land

Knowing the laws of the land will give you a foundational benchmark for your decision-making processes. When I was in the Navy, I visited many different countries. Each country had different laws for different things. It was our duty during our visits to obey the laws of the land and if we broke them, we would be tried by their courts and then tried again by military court. Therefore, before we visited each country our commanding officers conducted training on the laws we needed to be aware of. One example was the country's drinking age. If the drinking age was 18 in a country, then soldiers and sailors under 21 were allowed to drink, regardless of the drinking age of 21 in the United States. We were subject to the laws of their land.

I could use many examples, but knowing the laws of the land will assist you in making the right decisions. If you disagree with a law, then it is important to make your case, but it still does not give you the right to disobey the law. For example, I disagree with the drinking age law in the United States. I believe if someone is old enough to die for their country then they should be old enough to make a decision about the consumption of alcohol. But just because I disagree with the law does not give me the right to buy minors alcohol. If I did break the law, I would be subject to the penalties associated with it. It is important for those in a democratic society to trust the laws which have been voted on and to vote against the laws they don't agree with.

Laws are put in place to keep countries civilized. When laws are consistently disobeyed without repercussion, you have the beginning of an uncivilized society. Making the right choice when you disagree with a law takes courage and you will sometimes need to show courage against your own feelings and opinions when it comes to the laws of your land. One last note, however, is if laws are put in place which conflict with your moral, ethical, or religious beliefs, then you will need to decide if the law is worth breaking. I don't envy people who are put in this position, but there are definitely times where breaking a law is necessary to do what's right. One example is the Nazi's genocide of Jews.

Many Germans hid Jews in their homes to keep them from being sent to concentration camps. This was forbidden by the laws of their land, but those who did were willing to stand up against any punishment for what they believed to be right. This is an extreme scenario and I hope none of us are ever put in this kind of situation. But if we are, I hope we do the right thing. Be sure to spend time to know and understand the laws of your land.

Know your motivation for making decisions
Author and keynote speaker John Maxwell says, "Motivation is when you make decisions to benefit everyone. Manipulation is when you make decisions to only benefit yourself." If you are making decisions that only benefit you and others are hurt, underprivileged, or deceived, then you need to rethink your motivation. On the other hand, if you are making decisions which benefit everyone, including yourself, then you are choosing in the right direction. Too often people make decisions based on how it will benefit them and do not give a second thought to how their decisions will affect others. Many times people unintentionally hurt others by making self-centered decisions. It's not as if people sit around thinking, "how can I hurt others with my decisions." They simply do not consider the consequences their decisions could have on others.

The following two questions will help you make better decisions and live with fewer regrets. First, who will be affected by the decision I am about to make? Second, how will this decision affect those people? If you keep these questions in the forefront of your mind, it will help you make more decisions that are courageous towards what is right, just, and fair.

Know your fears
Fear is an unpleasant feeling of anxiety or apprehension caused by the presence or anticipation of danger. Fear causes people to do crazy things. Think for a moment what you would do if someone backed you into a corner and you were fearful for your life. You would probably

fight like you've never fought before and would most likely discover ninja moves you didn't know you had. Fear can be an excellent motivator if it is paired with courage. For example, parents make sure their children are dressed warm in the winter out of fear their kids may catch a cold, flu, or fever. The fear of failure can motivate people to prepare well for a speech, a sport, or a project. Knowing your fears will help you understand your reaction to fear, which will help you recognize when fear is affecting you mentally, physically or emotionally. When you recognize you are being affected by fear you can then use courage to defeat it.

COMMON FEARS

People fear snakes, spiders, death, heights, and flying, which are all valid fears. However, in this section, I would like to focus on active interpersonal fears. Active interpersonal fears are those you deal with in daily interactions which cause you to act and react in ways not aligned with your authentic self. As you recognize these fears within yourself, it is important to write them down and to evaluate how you should display courage in the face of these fears.

The Fear of Rejection

For most people, the fear of rejection starts from the experience of being rejected. Perhaps you expressed interest in a person and they told you they weren't interested. Perhaps you've had someone you love reject you. Perhaps you had a boss or teacher reject your work. Rejection hurts. I don't know a person who enjoys it, invites it, or promotes it, but rejection can be a great benefit to our self-image if we learn how to handle it properly. For example, consider what would happen if you asked someone out on a date and they turned you down. Would you decide to never again ask anyone else out on a date out of the fear of being rejected? What if your soul mate enters your life and you miss the opportunity to develop a relationship with that person for fear of being rejected? When we are faced with rejection, the natural tendency is to shut down. However, this response can cause us to miss out on the opportunities to have what we truly desire—in this case, a fulfilling romantic relationship. Courage enables you to face rejection and make the choice to try again, believing the prospect of being rejected is worth the risk of trying. What would happen if you were rejected by 10 people, and the tenth person you asked said 'yes' and it was the start of a fruitful, lifelong relationship? Would it be worth it? Absolutely! The courage to ask a 2nd, 3rd, and 4th time will give you confidence to overcome the fear of rejection and get what you desire.

A few symptoms of the fear of rejection:

- Limited creativity
- Reluctance to ask for something you truly desire
- The reluctance to share opinions or ideas

The Fear of Intimacy
Intimacy comes by being completely vulnerable with another person. Some people want to be vulnerable but refuse, especially if they have been hurt in the past. Additionally, people try to recreate intimacy experiences from the past instead of focusing on having intimacy in the present. You will often hear people talk about a past relationship where they experienced intimacy. Yet, they do not discuss the hurt or pain also associated with the relationship which now causes them to put up guards against being vulnerable. Intimacy is not about perfection; it is not about having euphoric feelings of closeness, infatuation, and joy all day, every day. Intimacy comes with pain. When you have been hurt by someone you are vulnerable with, it is important to admit it, give and receive forgiveness, and to be vulnerable again. The more you work through the pains of relational difficulty, the greater your level of intimacy will be.

A few symptoms of the fear of intimacy:

- Inauthentic behaviors

- Protective behaviors
- Loneliness

Fear of failure

The fear of failure is similar to the fear of rejection except it is focused on performance rather than relationships. Those who fear failure may see their performance as a way of gaining love and acceptance. In these cases, typically two things happen. One, a person who has performed well will not gain the love and acceptance they are looking for from a particular achievement. Therefore, they drive themselves to greater levels of achievements in hopes of gaining love and acceptance. Many people who are driven to achieve from fear of failure become depressed after achievements because the love and acceptance they receive does not equal their need. Two, a person will avoid performing for fear of losing the love and acceptance they have. They do not want to take risks because they are afraid if they fail, they will let others down. Therefore, they are reluctant to commit to new things and are afraid of stepping out of their comfort zone.

Symptoms of the fear of failure:

- Reluctance to commitment
- Overly competitive attitude
- Narcissistic behavior
- Underachievement
- Overachievement

Fear of looking foolish

The fear of looking foolish is the number one fear of human beings in active interpersonal settings. Statistically, the fear of public speaking is the number one fear. However, if you were to ask yourself why people fear public speaking, you'll discover the fear of looking foolish is the root cause. Think about it; why did you fear (if you didn't—you're rare!) giving a speech to your class when you were in middle school? It was because you knew if you made a mistake during your speech, you would be humiliated, made-fun-of, and laughed at by your peers. In short, you would look foolish.

I have found most active interpersonal fears to be rooted in the fear of looking foolish. This fear causes people to argue, procrastinate, attack, eliminate potential of risk, lie, cheat, overcompensate, underperform, hide their true self, and more. This fear shows up in specific ways for each of us. It is monumentally important for you to find out when, why, and how it shows up in your life. If you listen to your negative self-talk, you will hear it.

Symptoms of the fear of looking foolish:

- Lying to yourself and others
- Acting differently to fit in
- Social anxiety
- All other symptoms previously listed in other fears

Statistics on Fear
Knowing statistics on fear will help us understand when we should and should not give credence to our fears. The following statistics were gathered by the National Institute of Mental Health:

- 60% of our fears are totally unwarranted; they never come to pass.
- 20% of fears are focused on our past, which is out of our control.
- 10% of fears are focused on things so petty that they make no difference in our lives.
- Of the remaining 10%, only 4 to 5% of fears are justifiable.

I have heard people say fear is not real. I have heard people chastise others for things they have feared. I have been chastised for my fears. I don't know about you, but fear is pretty real to me. I have had physical, financial, social, and psychological fears and when the emotions hit me, fear has the ability to paralyze me. Fear is as real as we allow it to be. According to the statistics, however, when we give into fear, we are being duped 95% of the time. Giving into fear is one of the most counterproductive acts in life. When we give into fear, it causes us to not move forward in our lives. When we don't move forward in our lives, we don't gain understanding. When we don't gain understanding, we become ignorant and ignorance is a breeding ground for fear. Let us take the advice of Franklin Delano Roosevelt, "We have nothing to fear, but fear itself."

Courage is the antidote for fear. Eleanor Roosevelt said, "You gain strength, courage, and confidence by every experience in which you really stop to look fear in the face." The more we grow in courage, the stronger we become on the inside. The stronger we become on the inside, the less we will fear what is outside. Be sure to know, understand, and act upon what is right. Ask yourself how your decisions will affect yourself and others. Know the laws of your land and know your motivation for making decisions. Never forget that the cowardly people and the courageous people face the same fears. What they choose to do in the face of fear will determine what they become. Become courageous and choose to do what is right no matter the cost.

Become courageous and choose to do what is right no matter the cost.

CHECK POINT
Confidence is about standing on the truth, integrity, and rightness of who we are. Confidence doesn't compromise what is good, right, and

true for what is easy. Confidence comes with being teachable, honest, and courageous. You must take special care to build confidence with daily decisions made through character. Character will never disappoint you and as you make decisions towards the betterment of yourself and others, your self-image will become clearer and healthier. Inside of you is an authentic, confident, and courageous person needed by the world. Do not neglect to build your confidence. The world needs your gifts. Don't rob the world of you.

Step Three

Othermindedness

CHAPTER #17

What is Othermindedness

One of my favorite movies is *It's a Wonderful Life*. The movie is about George Bailey, a talented visionary who planned to leave his hometown of Bedford Falls to explore the world and build modern cities. After high school, George saved money for college and a trip to Europe by working for his father at the Bailey Building and Loan, a non-profit organization dedicated to helping the working class afford nice homes. The day before George left for his trip to Europe, his father had a stroke and passed away.

Mr. Potter, deemed "the richest man in town," owned nearly everything in Bedford Falls, including real estate and banks. Potter made a lot of money by charging extremely high rates for his poor quality homes. He despised the Building and Loan because it cut into his profits. After George's father passed away, Potter tried to shut down the Building and Loan. George knew many good people would be hurt if he allowed Potter to shut it down. So he gave up his dreams of travel and college to serve the people of Bedford Falls.

Over many years, George sacrificed college, a honeymoon, weekends, money, and more to help people fulfill their dreams. At times he became frustrated, but he never used his frustration to become selfish. He continued to serve regardless of the circumstances or personal loss. However, George struggled with feeling like a failure and feeling like his life didn't amount to much.

On Christmas Eve, George's Uncle Billy, who also worked at the Building and Loan, was supposed to deposit $8,000 (which would be the equivalent of $100,000 today), but on the way to depositing the money, he misplaced the envelope. Uncle Billy and George looked everywhere for the envelope but couldn't find it. George knew a lost envelope story wouldn't carry weight with law enforcement officials. He knew someone would go to jail for the lost money, and although he did not misplace the envelope, he was ready to once again serve by taking the blame. Sure enough, a bank auditor, an FBI agent, and a reporter began looking for George, having a warrant for his arrest

George went home panicky and frustrated. He quickly left again with intentions to commit suicide. When his wife Mary saw how distressed he was, she called Uncle Billy who told her what happened. Immediately, Mary went around Bedford Falls telling everyone she knew that George was in trouble. Right before George was about to attempt suicide, his guardian angel showed him how much his life affected others. After discovering what a wonderful life he had lived, George returned home to see his family. When he arrived home, he was met by Mary, with droves of people behind her. One by one people began dropping money in front of George while thanking him for all he had done for them. One of his oldest friends advanced him $25,000. All together George must have been given over $50,000 (Equivalent to nearly a million dollars today). During the giving frenzy, George's brother Harry called for a toast and said, "To my big brother George, the richest man in town!" George was not rich because of the money he received. He was rich because his life enriched so many other's lives.

Othermindedness (yes, it's a made up word) is thinking of others before yourself. It is, to paraphrase St. Paul, doing nothing out of selfish ambition or vain conceit, but in humility considering others better than yourself. It's looking not only to your own interests, but also to the interests of others. Statistics show that people think about themselves 95 percent of the time. This isn't necessarily wrong. We do everything with ourselves. We eat, sleep, shower, shave, and work with ourselves. It would be easy to look at the statistics and think this is negative, but when you look at the facts, we can't help but think of ourselves. Othermindedness is not about ridding yourself of all thoughts of you. It's about channeling your thoughts and actions towards the benefit of others.

Othermindedness is thinking of others before yourself.

CHAPTER #18
Hard Realities

People who struggle with self-image typically focus on themselves without thinking how their actions affect others. People with a negative self-image can become extremely self-conscious and selfish. They think every joke is an attack against them; they believe others focus on their mistakes or are worried about how they dress, perform, talk, walk, and chew their food. But the reality is people don't think about us an iota of the time we think about ourselves. Why? Because they are too busy thinking about themselves. When I learned this, it freed me in ways I never thought possible. I realized when I make mistakes, people think about it for a brief moment, they may even comment on it, but unless it directly affects their life, they forget it and move on. Never forget the following facts.

People rarely remember what you say
I know this especially well from being a teacher, speaker, and consultant. You can tell someone something you believe to be of vital importance. You can ask them to write it down and repeat it. You could even have them etch it in stone. Then the following week, you can ask them to repeat back what you spoke about and, unless it was im-

To connect with people, you must be otherminded.

portant to them, they probably won't remember. This is the big difference between communication and connection. To connect with people, you must be otherminded. You must ask yourself, "How can I make this message relevant to the person I'm speaking with?" If you don't, people will rarely remember what you say.

People sometimes remember what you do
Again, unless you do something that directly affects the other person, they will barely remember your actions, although they will remember

your actions more than your words. Now, if you do something epic like go streaking down the middle of a football field during a playoff game, people will remember that for a while. However, even in cases like that, over time, people will forget who did it, the location, and more. But if they were the one who went streaking, they would remember every detail and would probably tell the story for the rest of their lives. I'm also quite certain it would become an even greater story every time they told it.

People always remember how you make them feel
This is when your words and actions are rarely forgotten. Ask yourself this question: When is the last time someone made you feel foolish? Chances are you can remember the time, date, and location. How about this question: When is the last time someone made you feel really good about yourself? Chances are you can remember that as well. When directed towards the feelings of others, words have tremendous power. Words in the mouth of a hurtful person can be like flaming arrows which can pierce a heart, but words in the mouth of an otherminded person can bring healing, love, and life. Your actions, like your words, can also bring healing, love, and life when you intentionally use your gifts toward the betterment of others.

Never forget these three facts; they are essential to the foundation of othermindedness.

CHAPTER #19

Appreciation

Appreciation begins with sincerity. Dale Carnegie stressed sincerity in his timeless book, *How to Win Friends and Influence People*. "Flattery is from the teeth out. Sincere appreciation is from the heart out." You cannot fake appreciation; it is established by truly being grateful for everyone and everything in your life. Appreciation begins with a deliberate decision to focus on opportunity instead of obligation. When we focus on obligation, we often miss opportunities to make a difference in world. How often do people wake up and say, "Ugh, I have to go to (work, school, etc.) today," or "I hate (work, school, etc.), I wish I was sick so I could stay home." How many people who think like this make a difference in others' lives? Not many. What if instead they said, "I am so grateful I have a (job, school, etc.) where I can make a difference in the world." Focusing on opportunity instead of obligation does not mean there aren't things we don't like about work or school. Nobody ever said we have to enjoy every moment of every day, but focusing on opportunity instead of obligation will give you joy even in doing things you don't particularly enjoy. The good news is focusing on opportunity is a choice. It is essentially saying you are choosing hope, appreciation, and achievement over frustration, despair, and fear.

In my company's character and leadership school program, we help students focus on opportunity. Three of the most common phrases you will hear from middle and high school students are, "School sucks," "I hate school," and "I don't want to go to school today." First, we validate how the students are feeling. Then we tell them there are things about school that suck. We assure them there are things about school they won't like, and we promise them there will be days they won't want to come to school. Then we talk to them about the opportunity they have to shift their mindset from obligation to opportunity. We assure them that after school there will be things about their career they will dislike, and days they won't want to work. We challenge them to change these common phrases from obligation to opportunity. We have had students say, "I'm grateful I have the opportunity to go to school and be with my friends," and "I appreciate having the opportunity to learn," and "I'm going to focus on opportunity today." The students who follow through with this challenge see monumental changes in their attitude, grades, and friendships. We have received numerous letters from students thanking us for challenging them to change their mindset.

The science of appreciation

Appreciation is our body's natural combatant against fear, doubt, and worry. In our brains limbic system lies a synapse (the brains connection points) called the amygdala. The amygdala is the synapse which integrates our body with emotions, emotional behavior, and motivation. Emotional behavior is largely affected by the emotions of fear, doubt, and worry. If a large dog has chased you or you have given a speech in front of a big crowd, then you have felt the emotional effects of fear, doubt, and worry surging through your body. That is your amygdala firing sensations through your body to let you know something is wrong, but as we've discussed, 95 percent of our fear, doubt, and worry are unwarranted.

There are over six million people diagnosed with anxiety disorders in the United States alone and most patients receive prescription medication to help reduce the effects of their anxiety. Others turn to illegal drugs, alcohol, sexual addictions, tobacco, and other self-defeating crutches to counter the effects of the amygdala. Unfortunately, when the medicine wears off, the anxiety remains because the emotional behaviors remain. As the old saying goes, "If you do what you've always done, you'll get what you've always got." Unless we change emotional behaviors, we will always get the same emotional responses to fear, doubt, and worry. The good news is there is a way to naturally combat the negative emotions from the inside out.

According to Dr. Harold Bafitis, the amygdala cannot fire when you are in a state of appreciation. Being appreciative by finding opportunity instead of living out of obligation literally eliminates fear, doubt, and worry from our lives. Appreciation isn't just some fluffy topic meant to make you feel good for a short period of time. Appreciation is a natural drug to combat negative emotions, and the best part is, it comes without any negative side effects. If you discipline yourself in appreciation, you will physiologically change the way your body functions. In order to discipline yourself in appreciation, you must develop simple practices to remind yourself to be appreciative every day. Before I share these practices with you, I want to remind you again that discipline is never easy at first. It will take consistent effort for you to develop these practices, but it is worth it. As my mentor used to say, "Discipline weighs ounces and regret weighs tons." You will never regret the decision to be disciplined, especially once you've gained the rewards associated with it.

Appreciation is a natural drug to combat negative emotions, and the best part is, it comes without any negative side effects.

Appreciation practice

Every morning think of 25 things you're thankful for. This is a practice I began to develop 15 years ago. Every morning when I wake up, I begin to give thanks first for the people in my life, and then I think of ways I am thankful for each of them. For example, I give thanks for my wife Brittany. I say how thankful I am for her beauty, both inside and out. I am thankful for the way she loves me and our children unconditionally. I am thankful for her friendship and the way she makes me laugh. I am thankful for her belief in the possibilities and her belief in me. I am thankful for the way she studies and is never satisfied with status quo. I am thankful for the way she inspires me to be more of who I am.

As you can see, just one person can bring out numerous sub-categories for thankfulness which puts you in the state of appreciation. Giving thanks is one of the best ways to be otherminded. Just imagine how you would treat all of the people in your life if you consistently thought about how you are thankful for them. Trust me when I tell you this practice will change your life. After you have given thanks for all the people in your life, you can give thanks for your possessions, your career, your past, present, and future. To be honest, it is very difficult to get to 25 things because you can stay on one thing for an hour at a time. The point, however, is not to reach 25, but to get you into a consistent state of appreciation. Do this every day and you will see a remarkable difference in your attitude, focus, and creativity.

CHAPTER #20

Generosity

Generosity is from the Latin word generosus, which means "of noble birth." Throughout history people of noble birth belonged to a hereditary class with high social or political status. Isn't it a remarkable thought that by being generous, you put yourself in a higher social class? Unfortunately, truly generous people are far and few between because of the lies associated with generosity. In my company's training program, we have a discussion on the truths versus lies in generosity. Let's look at a few of these.

TRUTHS VS. LIES IN GENEROSITY
> **Truth** – People will hurt you.

> **Lie** – Protect yourself so no one will ever hurt you.

> **Truth** – You can be generous even if people hurt you.

> **Lie** – Hurting those who have caused you pain will help the pain go away.

> **Truth** – Being generous always yields a return on investment.

> **Lie** – If you give, you should always get something back.

> **Truth** – Giving is more than money; it is more generous to give of your time than money, because you can never get your time back.

> **Lie** – If you don't have money to give you can't be generous. If you don't have money, you're not good enough.

THE REAL TRUTH ABOUT GENEROSITY
Generosity is a choice. You can be generous with every decision you

make. You can choose to serve or be served. Generosity isn't an obligation; it's a blessing. You've heard the saying, "You can't take possessions with you when you die." Although the saying may not be true of your internal gifts and talents, you should still treat them in the same light. The more you give of yourself, the more you receive, and not all gifts have a bow and wrapping paper.

The more you give of yourself, the more you receive, and not all gifts have a bow and wrapping paper.

Many counselors and psychologists encourage patients struggling with depression to give of their time, serving less fortunate people because it instantly puts them in a state of appreciation. If you can give money, a great practice is to give anonymously. One practice I've developed over the years is paying for a random person's meal when going out to eat. I will ask the waiter or waitress to give me someone's bill and ask them not to tell who paid for their meal. Sometimes I will write an encouraging note and ask our server to give it to them. Occasionally I will hide and watch the people's reaction after I do this. It is amazing how people respond. I have watched people smile from ear to ear, I have seen people in complete disbelief, and I have even witnessed people cry from appreciation. I can tell you emphatically this practice puts me into a state of appreciation like none other. If you decide to do this, let me give you a little secret, breakfast and lunch prices are much cheaper, so if you don't have a lot of extra money that is a better place to start.

Another way to be generous is with your talents. I have a friend who is an excellent musician, songwriter, and singer. I used to joke and say he could pick up two sticks and a few rocks and play a beautiful piece of music. However, when we were younger, he was always hesitant to share his gifts with others for fear of looking showy. One evening I was urging him to pick up his guitar and sing something for me. After he refused me for the third time I finally said, "You're being selfish." He seemed offended by my comment, so I clarified. "Your gifts are meant to be given, when you play and sing it brings joy into my life." He soon picked up his guitar and played a new song that gave me goose bumps from head to toe. It was incredibly generous of him to share his gifts with me and I left his house that evening feeling inspired. Have you ever shared your talents and felt a feeling of euphoria from it? If you have, it is because you are giving, which instantly puts you in the state of appreciation. Giving of your talents should be a daily practice, but remember; as soon as you start giving out of obligation, you miss the opportunity because fear, doubt, and worry often accompany obligation. Give of your talents from your heart.

There are literally thousands of ways you can be generous with your time, talents, and treasures. The key is to find what being generous looks like for you and then give, give, and give some more.

CHAPTER #21

Smile...a lot

Years ago volunteers from a non-profit organization wanted to show people in their community how "love" looked in a practical way. They decided to buy cases of water, soda, and punch, put them in coolers of ice, and give them away for free on a hot summer day. Another thing they decided was not to promote their cause unless someone insisted. If people asked why they were giving away free drinks, they simply responded by saying, "We're just trying to show love in a practical way." The group received a mixed bag of responses. Some people were genuinely grateful, some people refused, some doubted the group's motives, some began asking more about their organization, and others merely took a drink and went on their way. There was one response they got that none of them would ever forget.

A middle-aged man with a sneer that could curdle dairy walked by and someone handed him a soda.

The man grabbed the soda and exploded, "I don't want to buy anything!"

The volunteer responded, "No sir, it's free; we're just trying to show love in a practical way."

The man sneered again, "Everyone always wants something from me, what game are you trying to play?"

The volunteer again responded, "Sir, I assure you, we don't want anything from you. We're just trying to show love in a practical way."

The man looked at the volunteer and said, "You all should have your heads examined! I demand to know what organization you're with."

The volunteer handed him a business card, he took it and his soda and walked on. When he walked about 30 yards, the man paused, looked down at his soda, and looked back at the volunteers, this time with a look of bewilderment. After his brief pause the man walked on.

Weeks later at the organization's headquarters, the man walked in with the soda can and the business card. A few of the volunteers recognized the man immediately and stopped what they were doing. After a moment of awkward silence, the man held up the soda can and demanded, "I want to know who is responsible for this." The volunteers quizzically looked at each other and someone finally told him they were all responsible for it. They explained to the man that the volunteers all got together and chose to give away free drinks in order to show love in a practical way. The man's face softened and he took a slight step back. He looked down for a brief moment and as he looked up his eyes were filled with tears. His lip slightly quivered as he again held up his can of soda, "I want you to know that this soda saved my life." The volunteer's eyes were fastened on him, but no one spoke. The man, while composing himself said, "The day you handed me this soda I was on my way to commit suicide, but after you handed me this I thought, 'If there are good people in the world like you, maybe life is worth living after all.'" That day the man became a faithful volunteer for their organization and to my knowledge, he still is to this day.

What's smiling got to do with it?
I've given away free drinks, free clothes, free books, and more. I wish I could give to more people, but it's not practical. I've firmly learned that giving is more an attitude of the heart than anything else, and an ancient proverb says, "Out of the abundance of the heart a person speaks." Remember, 55 percent of communication is body language, which can be specifically shown through facial expressions. Smiling at people is a simple way of showing people love in a practical way. You may think this is strange, but every time I walk into a grocery store, mall, school, company, symposium, or home I try to make a conscious effort to smile at people. Before going in, I remind myself of the soda-that-saved-a-life story and give my smile freely to everyone. A genuine smile tells a person, "You're something special." Sure, once in a while I smile at people who look at me like I'm weird, but most of the time when I smile

at people, they smile back. I've literally watched people's countenance change as a result of me smiling and them smiling back. Have you ever gone through a tough time and had someone give you a genuine, heartfelt smile? I have and I will tell you it is sometimes more refreshing than encouraging words.

The science of smiling
Genuine smiles stimulate our brain's reward mechanisms in a way that even chocolate, a well-regarded pleasure-inducer, cannot match. The endorphin release from smiling is similar to the endorphin release from exercise; it reduces stress, generates positive emotions, and puts us in the state of

Smiling is why people feel happier around children.

appreciation. Smiling is why people feel happier around children. Children smile on average of 400 times per day where the average adult smiles only 20 times per day. Just like frowning, smiling takes effort. However, it is scientifically proven it takes more effort to frown than smile, but it doesn't stop people from working hard on their frown. Be sure to work harder on your smile than your frown.

Smiling is such an easy way to be generous. Paired with the added bonus of how it benefits you physiologically, smiling regularly should be a no-brainer. Just keep in mind every time you walk into a store, mall, school, or any other type of organization that your smile can save a life. Say "Cheese!"

CHAPTER #22
Develop Sympathy, Empathy, and Compassion

Some of us are skilled in sympathy, others are good with empathy, and others are competent in compassion, but it is uncommon to find people who are successful in all three. To be otherminded, you must develop your sympathy, empathy, and compassion.

Sympathy

Sympathy is the ability to enter into, understand, or share someone else's feelings. Sympathy is based upon your concern for the well-being of others. You practice sympathy when you have not experienced what someone else is experiencing. For example, if you are at a funeral for a friend who has lost a loved one and you have never lost a loved one, you can show sympathy by doing your best to put yourself in their shoes. You might ask yourself: "How would I feel if I lost a loved one? What emotions would I be feeling? What would I want others to do for me?" From these questions, you can sympathetically comfort your friend, yet unless you have gone through a similar experience, you will not understand the full measure of their pain. Nevertheless, do not underestimate the power of sympathy. Your experiences don't have to be the same as others to show love and grace to those who are struggling. Develop sympathy and use it well.

Empathy

Empathy is the ability to identify with and understand somebody else's feelings or difficulties. Empathy is based upon mutual understanding and concern for the well-being of others. You practice empathy when you have experienced what someone else is experiencing. For example, let's say you and a friend are working for an oppressive leader who constantly criticizes you for making mistakes. When your friend is criticized for a mistake she made, you are able to empathize with her feelings because you have also experienced criticism. You can use empathy to tell your friend you understand what they are going through and help them maintain a positive self-image in spite of their struggle. You can remind yourself how you felt when you were criticized by asking these questions:

- How did I feel when I went through this?
- What were my emotions?
- What helped me get through the emotional difficulty?

Empathy is a great tool for understanding, grace, and love.

Compassion
Compassion means co-suffering. However, compassion moves past sympathy and empathy from the stage of understanding and into a desire to help others during their suffering. Compassion alleviates suffering by taking action. For example, let's say a friend of yours is struggling financially. You sympathize and empathize with them, but you go a step further by paying a few bills for them and giving them extra money for groceries. Once you take action, you are having compassion for them; you are literally taking their burdens on yourself. Compassion can be shown in many ways. If you see a mother with four kids at the grocery store and she is having a hard time getting her groceries in her car, you can help her put in her groceries. You can show compassion by giving someone a hug, buying them flowers, or helping them move furniture. Remember, the major difference between sympathy and empathy versus compassion is action.

COMBINING SYMPATHY, EMPATHY, AND COMPASSION
A Chinese proverb says, "To understand is hard, but once one understands, action becomes simple." Understanding and action work hand in hand. As I said earlier,

The more you help others, the less you think about yourself.

emotion is one of the most powerful forces in the world. When we are emotionally connected to a person in their suffering, we are compelled to help them; this goes right back into the difference between obligation and opportunity. Emotional connection to someone's suffering (sympathy and empathy) compels us towards the opportunity to help (compassion). I cannot stress enough how important this is to building a positive self-image. The more you help others, the less you think about yourself. As you emotionally put yourself into the sufferings of others, the less power suffering will have over you simply because you won't be focused on your personal struggles. Also, when we are engaged in helping others, the magnitude of our own problems tends to "shrink" as we connect and share in the lives of others.

Throughout the years, I have witnessed parents, teachers, coaches, students, and leaders ignore love shown through sympathy, empathy, and compassion in order to "fix" people's problems. People don't need to be fixed—they need to be loved. Too often people are careless with other people's feelings when they are going through difficulty and they end up causing greater stress on a person's situation. Let me ask you a question: Have you ever gone through a tough time and expressed your feelings to someone only to have them cut you off and start giving you advice? How did that make you feel? Unappreciated, unloved, or disregarded? Did you need advice or did you simply need sympathy, empathy, or compassion?

I have learned through mentoring and coaching that most people know what they need to do solve their problems. When we give people un-warranted advice we actually cause greater confusion and frustration. Advice should only be given when it's asked for. Even then, you might want to ask more questions before offering your opinion on the situation. Remember this proverb, "A fool finds no pleasure in understanding, but delights in airing his own opinion." Take time to develop the following skills of sympathy, empathy, and compassion and you will avoid giving free and unwarranted advice.

A REAL-LIFE EXAMPLE OF SYMPATHY, EMPATHY, AND COMPASSION
Years ago I received a letter from a young man who was, at the time, in despair. In order to give you context, I am going to share the letter with

you. I've received permission from this young man to use the letter. I have changed his name and have left out a few parts of the letter to protect his identity. Besides those few changes, the letter is in its raw state. As you read, please understand that his story—while tragic—is not as uncommon as I wish it were.

Dear Mr. Ross,

My name is John Doe. I am 15 years old. I attend a local school. I was made aware that you visit another local school once per week. I am very good friends with some people that attend that school, and they told me about you. Well, let me give you my story. Since the beginning of 5th grade, I started to receive badgering, threats, and malicious comments made toward me. At first, I shrugged it off, not worrying about other people and how they decided to treat me, because I thought it would go away in due time. Well, the situations began to escalate. The badgering started as once a day, but it quickly became 12 to 14 times per day. I started to take to heart what these people began to say. I began to hate myself. I looked into the mirror one day and saw myself as hideous, worthless, and almost as a cancer to society.

My father was the biggest reason that I was like this. He was a heavy alcoholic, and he had a tendency to get drunk a lot. One day, he got drunk and for whatever reason, he beat on me. I had no idea what I had done, and to this day, I still don't know why he had been set off. He is no longer a drinker, as he has not had alcohol for almost 2 years now. But that does not change his behavior on the behalf of aggression. He began to scream at me for the smallest things.

It wouldn't be the usual disciplinary scream that a child would get for knocking over an expensive vase. No, these were of great malice, as he would tell me I am worthless, a mistake, and accident. He would tell me that he did not love me. He told me multiple times that he would drop me off in the middle of nowhere because he hated me so much. He tells me all the time how he wants to knock my teeth down my throat. I am very concerned that he might do it one day. I keep a knife in my room just in case he really does decide to try. I really don't want to do it, but in the heat of the situation, it is the only thing I have to defend myself. He always gets in my face, makes degrading remarks, and it is always very constant. About 2 to 4 times per day he says these things.

Well, a few summers ago I began to self-harm. I started by hitting myself until I bruised. I then got into knives, razors, etc. I cut myself for a while. Then one day, I stumbled across a lighter. I started by getting a paper clip, and heating that and applying the heated object to myself. I then accidentally burned myself directly, and I began doing that. I no longer use the lighter, but I am still afraid I might start again. Over the course of this time, I have attempted suicide 6 times. I found no reason for my existence. I had planned it numerous more times, but I thought of everyone that it would affect. The most recent of my attempts was in a grouping of 3 times, which were about a month ago. All of these attempts were planned so that I would suffocate myself. They did not work, as I am here, but from time to time, I wish that it did.

My best friend, Jane Doe, asked me to contact you. She said she came up to you last week and spoke somewhat about me. She gave me your email, and told me that I should send you an email. For 5 days I just couldn't do it. I lack trust for anyone other than a very certain few, and I was very hesitant to write you this email. But she told me she was going to try talking to you about this, so I decided it would be best to send you this, telling you about me. I talk myself down from hurting myself every day. I am collapsing. She is my biggest support, and she is the closest thing to real family that I have.

I don't want to end it all because I wouldn't want to put that burden on her shoulders, but at the same time, if things get bad enough, then I am not sure if that would stop me or if it would just slow me down. I have heard so many great things about you, and I don't really know who else to talk to.

Thank you for your time and patience.

Sincerely,
John Doe

After reading this letter, I was moved to tears. I wanted to make sure I responded with sympathy, empathy, and compassion. I also wanted to make sure I could speak to his love language the best I could. After reading his letter numerous times, I responded. In parenthesis I will show where I used sympathy, empathy, and compassion.

John Doe,

First, I want to thank you for being so brave. I want you to know that I understand how hard it is to talk about deep issues (empathy) and I admire you for doing this. You have proven by doing this that you are unique. Most people never admit they struggle and never find freedom.

Second, I want to encourage you. I'm so sorry that you've felt worthless, hideous, and as a cancer to society (sympathy). I'm so sorry that your classmates treated you so poorly. I'm so sorry that your dad has treated you with such disregard (sympathy). I want you to know something--NONE OF THOSE THINGS ARE A REFLECTION OF WHO YOU ARE.

You, my friend, are a masterpiece. There's nothing about you that is worthless, hideous, or a cancer. There is something inside of you that is dying to get out. Please John, stay with those of us who are desperate to hear and see what's inside of you (compassion). With all of the things you've been through, I understand it's hard to trust (empathy). I understand your want to give up (empathy). All of your feelings are valid.

However, the world needs John Doe. The world needs what YOU and ONLY YOU can offer us. The way I see it is this: Those who have had it the hardest have the most to give. You, John Doe, have a story...a story that I want to see unfold...let me help you in your journey....I'm here to help (compassion).

My contact info is xxx.xxx.xxxx. You can call me or text me anytime. I would like to meet with you if you're willing to do that (compassion). If I can be of help to you in anyway...I want to be there.

Don't hesitate to contact me. Thank you again for your bravery. Everything gets better from here...

Michael B. Ross

After a few conversations with this young man, I learned his love language was words of affirmation. I made sure I said as many kind and encouraging words as I could. He later reported back to me that the encouragement had changed his life. He said he could not believe someone who did not know him well would believe in him and he was starting to believe in himself. Years have gone by and although he still has his struggles, he is beginning to develop a positive self-image and overcome the pain of his past. His situation at school has turned around, and while he still has his struggles at home, he is able to channel his emotions in healthier, more productive ways.

CHAPTER #23
Listen Intently

Hearing is to perceive a sound made by someone or something. Listening is to give attention to the person speaking. Hearing is focusing on your thoughts, ideas, or opinions. Listening is focusing on someone else's thoughts, ideas, or opinions. Hearing is self-focused and listening is others-focused. Our ongoing self-talk makes listening one of the most difficult practices to master. To be a great listener you must quiet your self-talk and discipline your mind to focus on the other person. Listening is one of the most valuable skills in any market. Great listening is the number one skill of great leaders. The following practices will help you become a great listener.

> To be a great listener you must quiet your self-talk and discipline your mind to focus on the other person.

Quiet your self-talk

I have three small children who clamor for my attention. Since I do a lot of work from home, they often interrupt me while I'm intently focused on something. They say things like, "Daddy, can you play with me?" or "Can you get me a drink?" Sometimes they interrupt me during a coaching or conference call, which is cute, but not appropriate. Our self-talk is sometimes like my children; it will interrupt you at the most inopportune times. One phrase I use to quiet my self-talk while listening is, "This is the most important person in the world right now." This includes me, background noise, people walking by, and any other distraction vying for your attention. Sometimes I have to repeat the phrase again and again until my mind becomes intently focused. By doing this I shift from hearing to listening. Practice this phrase and quiet your self-talk.

Ask another question

There is an ancient saying, "Be quick to listen, slow to speak, and slow to become angry." In nearly every conversation, there are moments when you will want to jump in and share your opinion. Instead, discipline yourself to ask another question. When you do this, you will keep the focus on the other person, you will have greater understanding, and when it is time for you to share, your words will be more powerful.

Take a deep breath
Conversations often have awkward silences, especially if someone is talking about a deep personal issue. The tendency for the listener is to start talking in order to fill the awkward silence. Instead, look the person in the eyes, take a deep breath, and slightly nod your head in the "yes" motion. Nine times out of ten the other person will begin speaking again. Typically, when they begin speaking again they will divulge much more information the second time around.

These practices work wonders in helping you gain greater understanding and depth in relationships. Quiet your self-talk, ask more questions, and take a deep breath to build a better self-image. Listen closely.

CHAPTER #24
Thoughtfulness

Thoughtfulness is treating people in a kind and considerate way, especially by anticipating their wants or needs. Steve Jobs, the founder of Apple, was a master at this. He thoughtfully considered what people wanted before they said they wanted it. He designed systems, phones, and computers by thinking about how he could make people's lives simpler and more fun. As a result, Apple has created and designed some of the greatest products in the world.

To be thoughtful, you must understand the wants or needs of an individual. Author Gary Chapman wrote a book called *The 5 Love Languages*. I highly recommend this book for anyone who has not read it and for those who have, I recommend you constantly refresh yourself in it. In the book, Dr. Chapman breaks down five ways people express love emotionally. Each person has a primary love language and to care for a person properly, we must learn their language. By knowing a person's love language, you will be able to discern how to be thoughtful towards them. The following is a list of paraphrased descriptions of each love language from the book.

Words of Affirmation
This involves providing honest, authentic, genuine, and focused compliments and positive, affirming words of encouragement. These help build another's self-image and confidence.

Quality Time
This is when you show someone how much they mean to you by setting aside special time with your full and undivided attention.

Gifts
People with this language feel loved by receiving and giving any type of gift, large and small.

Acts of Service
With this language, people feel like you truly care for them when you go out of your way to serve them by completing activities without being asked.

Physical Touch
A person with this language feels loved by a simple touch on the shoulder, a pat on the back, or a hug.

Although everyone has a primary love language, everyone feels love on some level with each language. Therefore, we still need to do our best to display care for people in each area. By asking questions and using listening skills, you will be able to identify a person's love language. Thoughtfulness is a pro-active approach to sympathy, empathy, and compassion. Thoughtfulness anticipates what a person wants or needs. When you act on behalf of a person's wants and needs, you will be able to make a resounding impact in their lives. Ultimately, this will lead you towards a better self-image.

> **When you act on behalf of a person's wants and needs, you will be able to make a resounding impact in their lives.**

CHAPTER #25

Coach, Mentor, and Teach

Where are you in your journey of building a positive self-image? Do you find yourself in a place where you are ready to build up and encourage others? One of the most gratifying and life-giving practices is to help people overcome struggles similar to the struggles we've overcome. As you read the following testimony of what it's like to coach, mentor and teach others, be sure to consider where you are at with your struggles. The last thing you should do is begin mentoring someone if you are deeply struggling with an issue in your self-image. When I was young, I asked someone to mentor me. I believed he had it together. After our first meeting, I realized I was wrong. He had numerous issues he was struggling with and I ended up mentoring him. Although it was great experience for me, the man was in no state to mentor someone else. Make absolutely sure your self-image is in a healthy state prior to entering in to mentoring. Yes, mentoring will build your self-image, but you must have your foundation in place before you start building.

If you are at a place where you feel ready, then take action. As you will notice from the following story, there are too many hurting people in the world for you to read this and do nothing.

Mentoring—A life-giving practice

It was the largest crowd I'd ever spoken in front of. I was nervous so I kept looking over my notes to make sure I wouldn't forget anything. As they announced my name, I reminded myself of why I was there—to inspire young men and women to live fulfilled and impactful lives. I delivered a powerful message by sharing my story and challenging students to live with character as a way to counteract negative self-image. I spoke about drugs, bullying, and suicide and told the students if they needed to talk, I would be there for them. At the end of the assembly, you could hear a pin drop. I knew the message had sunk in. What happened afterwards would change my life.

A young man was standing by the gym entrance pacing back and forth after all the other students were gone. He looked unsure of himself and he kept looking at the door as if he was contemplating walking out. I walked up to him, shook his hand, and introduced myself, "Hi buddy, my name is Michael."

He firmly shook my hand and said, "I'm Joe."

I leaned on a nearby wall and said, "What's going on Joe? How did you like the assembly?"

He looked me straight in the eyes and said, "It was good..." Tears flooded his eyes, "...your story really touched me. I've got to tell you something, but I don't want you to tell anyone else."

I put my arm on his shoulder and said, "I can't promise anything Joe, but you can trust that I want what's best for you."

That seemed to satisfy him and he took a deep breath and said, "I've been planning my suicide for months. Everyone thinks I'm a freak and most days I wonder why I'm alive. I try to fit in but it seems like no matter what I do I make myself look like more of a freak. I figure the world is better off without me and I just haven't worked up the courage to kill myself."

I was filled with sympathy and compassion and after thinking for a moment, I grabbed both of his shoulders and said, "Joe, please don't kill yourself. I tell you what; I'm going to be here for the next 9 weeks. Would you eat lunch with me on the days I'm here?"

A slight smile cracked the corner of his lips, "Yes."

To be honest with you I didn't know what I was going to do. I've had extensive training in mentoring, teaching, and coaching, but training and the real thing are two totally different things. I decided just to spend time with him, encourage him, and to take his focus off the areas he considered weaknesses.

The next week, I went to meet Joe for lunch; I spotted him at a table all by himself with his back to the other students. I waved to him to make sure he knew I was there and went through the line to get my lunch. As I was waiting for my food, I saw a group of students laughing and carrying on at a table near Joe. One of the students threw a carrot and hit Joe in the back. Joe didn't move or react, almost as if to say he deserved it. Anger filled my heart in a way I'd rarely experienced. It was the anger of injustice and it was justified. I grabbed my tray, picked up the carrot, walked over to the students with a slight smile on my face and dropped the carrot on their table.

I then glared at each student for a moment and said, "You guys dropped something." Then I put one hand on their table and pointed at the student who threw the carrot and said, "I suggest you never drop anything ever again!"

Joe had been watching the scene from the corner of his eye and when I sat down I could see the appreciation on his face. "So how are you?" I asked with a smile. He smiled back and began conversing with me.

Over the next few weeks, I had the privilege of spending time with this remarkable young man. He was highly intelligent, well spoken, and creative. During our fifth meeting he brought me a science fiction novel he had been working on. It was really good! I encouraged him to write more and to share his novel with others. I encouraged him on how smart and funny he was. I encouraged him to attend a youth summit I was a part of and reassured him that he would be accepted and loved. My time with Joe was enjoyable, and I was shocked he didn't have a lot of friends. Perhaps it was because he dressed differently, had an advanced sense of humor, or had an extensive vocabulary. Regardless of the reason, Joe had felt worthless and thought his life didn't amount to anything. On the final week, I was again encouraging Joe on how great he was. I told him his future was bright and spoke with him about his future plans. During the middle of our conversation, Joe stopped and looked down at the table for a long moment.

Then he looked up at me and said, "You know Michael, nobody ever says anything nice to me. Thank you."

Joe and I finished our meetings together with jokes, laughs, and a warm hug. I'm happy to report Joe is in college pursuing his passion. He sees his value in direct opposition to the way he saw it the first day we met. He now knows he is a masterpiece and he is going to use his gifts to benefit the world.

I can honestly tell you I did not do anything special with Joe. I simply ate lunch with him, listened, and gave him positive feedback. Does this make me special? No. Does it make me different? Yes. Most people didn't give Joe a chance. They wrote him off as a "weirdo" and avoided him at all costs. One thing I know from being a business/life coach, consultant, and speaker is there are a lot of "Joe's" out there. I've spoken with hundreds of people who see themselves as worthless freaks that don't see how their life matters.

This isn't limited to school-aged students; I could give you story after story of people who I've spoken with—business owners, teachers, coaches, supervisors, parents, and more— who feel just like Joe did. You may have rolled your eyes at the statistic that 85 percent of adults struggle with a negative self-image, but I'm here to testify, it's accurate. The problem with wounded adults is the older they get, the more skilled they become at masking their negative self-image. Their coping mechanisms become routine, and as creatures of habit, human beings can habitually steer themselves away from their best life by not confronting their wounds. Most of the people you work with, go to school with, play racquetball with, and live with are struggling with self-image.

My challenge to you is to mentor someone with the intentions of drawing out the lies in their life, and encouraging them towards a better self-image. It doesn't have to be anything formal. You just need to find time to meet with someone on a regular basis. I've met people for coffee, to shoot hoops, to hit softballs, or to play games, play guitar, or discuss a book. The venue isn't as important as your personal mission for meeting with them. As I've said, nothing will build your self-image greater than helping someone else build their self-image. We retain 30 percent of the information we are taught and retain 50 percent of the information we write about. However, we retain 90 percent of the information we teach others. Does this mean you have to be a professor to help someone else? No. As you meet with someone and begin to learn about their struggles, you will be compelled to help them find answers. Using the principles from the earlier sections of this book will help guide you as you meet. Your presence is the greatest present. You don't need to have everything figured out; you just need to be consistent.

Your presence is the greatest present.

Mentoring is a true win-win situation. You will win by being motivated to learn, practicing the skills of othermindedness, and seeing a life impacted by your presence. Your protégé will win by having someone to rely on; learning the steps to positive self-image, and having someone encourage them towards action. Take your knowledge, experiences, and beliefs and pour them into another life. Never forget, your presence is the greatest present. Give it away.

CHECK POINT
Othermindedness is thinking better of others than yourself. It's amazing what happens to our self-image when we get outside of ourselves and focus on the lives of others. Appreciation is the first step. Don't forget to think of 25 things you are thankful for. As you do this, then fear, doubt, and worry will begin vacating your life. Develop sympathy, empathy, and compassion. Remember to listen well and be thoughtful in your interactions with others. Finally, find someone to mentor. Nothing will bring more joy to your life than helping someone else develop the power of a positive self-image.

Can you imagine what the world would be like if everyone was otherminded? I don't know about you, but I'd like to find out. I'll be otherminded for you, you be otherminded for me. Let's see what happens.

CHAPTER #26

So Now What?

My brilliant professor Dr. Maureen Vanterpool used to ask her students, "So now what?" after we had a stimulating discussion, wrote a great paper, or gave a powerful speech. Her point was very simple: None of this means anything if we don't take action. It is the application of our education that makes the biggest difference in our lives. I use this as the title of this chapter to honor her, but also because it is relevant to us all. Let me present it like this, "So now ..." I have done my best to give you tools—that if practiced—will lead you to a positive self-image. Yes, we need to take action, but allow me to say this: You are valuable beyond measure whether or not you take any action. The action will lead you towards a better life, but it does not define your worth or value.

I would, however, implore you to take action because you're worth it, not because someone is telling you to or pushing you. Take action because with a positive self-image, the possibilities are endless. Take action because you are a masterpiece waiting to be chiseled out. Take action because there are others out there who need you. Take action because your gifts, talents, and abilities have the power to change the world.

The foundation of your self-image rests on what you to believe to be true about yourself. Truly believing that you have inherent worth and value will motivate you to put in the efforts necessary to uproot negative thought processes about yourself and your life. This, in turn, will develop into a lifestyle of self-respect that honors and encourages others. What you believe about yourself will show up in your actions and your actions will shape your life.

What you believe about yourself will show up in your actions and your actions will shape your life.

When you tear down the beliefs associated with a negative self-image and build a life of character and confidence, the impossible becomes possible. Believe in yourself, believe in the possibilities, and believe in the truth. Build your confidence with character. Become otherminded in all you do. Each of these actions will hammer away at the pieces in your life that don't represent who you really are. Eventually, the masterpiece inside you will emerge in a way that will have people marveling at your greatness.

I hope they all get a clear view.

MICHAEL B. ROSS

SPEAKER

A Better Life
PODCAST

mainstream
lifesolutions

For more
opportunities to
connect with
Michael B. Ross,
find us on
Facebook and
Twitter

AUTHOR

MICHAEL ROSS

Coach

OVERCOMING
THE CHARACTER
DEFICIT

HOW TO RESTORE AMERICA'S
GREATNESS ONE DECISION AT A TIME

OVERCOMING THE
CHARACTER DEFICIT
Student Guide

MainstreamLS.com

"Helping
People Live
Fulfilled and
Impactful
Lives"

Made in the USA
Monee, IL
01 March 2020